RY

Building the Real-Time Enterprise

An Executive Briefing

MICHAEL HUGOS

WILEY

John Wiley & Sons, Inc.

Contents

To Bunny, Joe, and Chloey

Preface

It is abundantly clear that our world is now shaped on a moment-to-moment basis by the rising flow of data that instantly records events happening anywhere and reports them to people everywhere. This phenomenon is giving rise to what we call the "real-time" world. It is a world where actions and their consequences follow one another closely and quickly. Wrong choices and inappropriate behaviors seem to bring on more and more trouble faster and faster. And effective choices and appropriate behaviors deliver success in greater and greater amounts just as quickly. What a roller coaster!

Now, more than ever, people and organizations need ways to make sense of and navigate through this real-time world. In my business career over the last 20 and some years, I have thought about these issues and had the opportunity to apply my ideas to actual operations and projects. From my experience, I find the ideas that are most useful and work most often rely heavily on the concepts of cybernetics and general systems theory.

I first came across these concepts while I was an undergraduate student at the University of Cincinnati. I was studying architecture and city planning and looking for some way to tie together information from disciplines such as engineering, economics, sociology, and design. I began to run across names like Jay Forrester, Norbert Wiener, and Stafford Beer. I read their books and their ideas became the framework that I used to organize and make sense of all the facts and techniques that were taught in my university courses.

That framework created in Cincinnati has stayed with me since then. I continue to update it through experience and it becomes more accurate and useful as time goes by, which leads me to believe that frameworks based on cybernetics and general systems theory are very effective ways to look at and operate in the real-time world.

I am a business executive who has gotten really good at deploying information technology to help companies cut costs, increase productivity, and exploit new revenue opportunities. I've seen and learned much about what works and what does not. I've sifted through blizzards of computer industry research and business management reports. I've talked with and read the works of people who have also experienced and thought deeply about these issues.

This book is an executive level presentation on how to understand and build a real-time enterprise. I know you are busy. I have made every effort to be as succinct, to the point, and clear as possible.

MICHAEL HUGOS

Chicago, Illinois
May 2004

Acknowledgments

I am the chief information officer (CIO) of Network Services Company (*www.nsconline.com*). The company is a multibillion distribution organization that provides customers across North America with foodservice disposables, janitorial supplies, printing paper, and related supply chain services. I would like to acknowledge Network Services for providing opportunities over these last several years to design and build systems that are proving to be very effective competitive tools for the company. I have been able to apply my ideas and continuously improve them through real-life experience.

I want to thank the managers and staff in the IT group at Network Services. They have all been collaborators with me in the design, building, and operation of the systems we created. They each are skilled at what they do and they routinely go beyond the call of duty to ensure that our systems are built successfully and that they operate reliably. They make me look good.

I wish to acknowledge Carolyn Ryffel. Carolyn is a cross-cultural trainer who works with people in multinational organizations and teaches them to function effectivley in different countries and cultures. She has provided me with many insights about organizational behavior and in numerous conversations she has described how people in different cultures think and respond. She has helped me make this book relevant to people around the world, not just in North America.

I would also like to acknowledge my editor Tim Burgard at John Wiley & Sons. This is the second book I have done with him. A few years ago he picked out my proposal and writing sample from among the many that he reviews every month. He recognized some raw talent for writing clearly and explaining things and he gave me an opportunity to write my first book. Then in conversations and e-mails last year he helped me to define the subject matter and content for this book. Thank you, Tim.

CHAPTER 1

The Promise of the Real-Time Enterprise

We are in the stage of our economy where the fusing together of information technology and business operations is creating what has come to be called the *real-time enterprise*. Computers have been widely used in business for the last four decades, but what is happening now is something new. A wide array of information technology is being custom tailored and fine-tuned to fit people's precise needs. The real-time enterprise is an organization in which specific and relevant information—not just an indiscriminant flood of data—flows continuously to individual people throughout the organization. They use this information hour by hour, day to day, and week to week to perform their jobs at levels of efficiency and responsiveness not possible before.

Every well-rounded executive is expected to understand the essentials of finance, operations, marketing, and sales. Now every well-rounded executive also needs to understand the essentials of applying information technology (IT) to address common business problems. The rise of the real-time enterprise makes the use of IT central to a company's survival and success.

Executives can no longer allow themselves to be bewildered by technical discussions about information systems. They must be able to apply a basic understanding of how to use IT in business so that they can make their own assessments of existing and proposed information systems. They can no longer rely entirely on the advice of outside experts in this area.

There are technical specialists who build and operate computer systems just as there are accountants who keep a company's books, factory managers who run a company's factories, and salespeople who find customers for a company's products. The executive does not need to know all the details involved in each of these activities. What is necessary is that the executive understands enough about all of them to see how they work together and provide the company with its ability to profitably deliver products and services to its customers.

This book lays out the key concepts needed to effectively use information technology to create and sustain a real-time enterprise. The concepts are presented in the form of a business briefing. This chapter and the next one provide an overview of the main business issues and scientific foundations that underpin the real-time enterprise. The next four chapters then discuss how company structures and ways of doing business are changing as the full impact of IT is now being felt. The remaining chapters talk specifically about how an effective executive can identify the need for and oversee the development of the systems required to move their company into the real-time world.

DEFINITION OF THE REAL-TIME ENTERPRISE

A useful analogy is to think about the spread of electric power in the first decades of the twentieth century. Electricity was wired into factories, offices, and homes. The buildings themselves and the activities that could occur within those buildings changed profoundly as this happened. At first, the use of electricity for lighting, heating, and driving elevators, machines, and appliances was wondrous and amazing. Then it became the norm. We now expect buildings to be wired for electric power and most of us would hardly know how to operate in a building that did not have electricity.

A similar thing is happening with the spread of real-time IT. The nearly instantaneous delivery of information that this technology makes possible is changing the way organizations operate. Companies are leveraging and adding to their existing systems infrastructure to create real-time systems. Existing systems provide a foundation of basic business functionality, and this is being combined with new information technology to create systems that enable companies to sense and respond immediately to important events in their environments. This may seem wondrous and amazing but it will soon enough be the norm.

Gartner, a prominent research firm that focuses on business and technology, defines the idea of the real-time enterprise as an organization that "achieves competitive advantage by using up-to-date information to progressively remove delays in the management and execution of its critical business processes."[1] Gartner goes on to point out that their definition has no explicit reference to technology. The reason for this is that the central concept of the real-time enterprise is not about technology, even though IT is the enabler that allows a company to become real-time. Instead, the central concept is about continuously improving key business processes and adapting them to changing circumstances so that they deliver better value to customers and more profit to the company.

THE PACE OF CHANGE CONTINUES TO ACCELERATE

Let's take a quick look at the sequence of events that has brought about the real-time business world that is growing up around us. Since the start of the Industrial Revolution, the pace of change in business and the global economy has been steadily increasing. During the twentieth century several waves of innovation propelled the pace of change to move even faster. The introduction of the assembly line by Henry Ford and others in the early 1900s gave rise to the modern consumer society by delivering huge quantities of mass-produced items at prices that most people could afford.

As people became used to the availability of basic products such as cars, appliances, and clothes, they developed a demand for more specialized products with particular features that more closely met their needs and desires. Companies responded to this by defining market segments and developing a corporate structure in which separate divisions were created to focus on producing and selling products to each market segment. General Motors is a classic example of this. Instead of one company selling cars to a mass market, it became a collection of businesses selling different kinds of cars to different groups of customers. This structure became the model for business organizations everywhere.

Operations research techniques and continuing improvements in technology fueled a steady competitive race between companies during the 1950s, 1960s, and 1970s. In the 1980s, Japanese companies like Toyota employed the techniques of lean manufacturing and changed the way manufacturing is organized and performed around the world. The production process got faster, more efficient, and more responsive.

During the 1990s, computer and communications technology developed to the point where the real-time organization started to move from theory to reality. Just as lean manufacturing changed the way manufacturing is done, the principles and practices of the real-time enterprise are starting to change the way companies are organized and how they operate.

In the last 20 years we have seen long-established manufacturing companies fade away because they were unable to successfully adopt lean manufacturing techniques and thus could no longer compete. In the next 20 years we will see other organizations fade away because they cannot make the transition to real time. Those organizations that do succeed in becoming real-time enterprises will need to change dramatically in the process.

This is a genuine wave of change, not just another IT fad. The real-time enterprise comes about through the use of IT but it is not about IT. The wealth-generation capabilities inherent in real-time operations are the major force that is driving this change. The switch over to real-time operations and the building of systems infrastructures to support this will be a major economic driver for the next several decades. This process has just begun and will accelerate as companies that become adept at real-time operations demonstrate the results that are possible from this way of operating.

WHAT DOES A REAL-TIME ENTERPRISE DO?

A real-time organization is a company that has learned to operate in a continuously changing and coordinated manner with its suppliers and customers. A real-time organization receives, analyzes, and acts on a steady stream of information that describes its market environment and its internal operations. It is both constantly fine-tuning the efficiency of its internal operations and watching for and responding to new opportunities in the markets it serves.

Real-time enterprises are replacing the traditional Industrial Age organization that works on a monthly, quarterly, or yearly management cycle. Reaction times are too slow in those organizations. They follow management practices that arose from a time when most information traveled on paper, a cup of coffee cost a nickel, and the business world moved at a much slower pace.

The competitive playing field now requires that companies are more aware of their performance and their markets on a daily or even hourly basis so that they are able to maximize their internal operating efficiencies, spot new opportunities, and respond to them quickly. Real-time organizations enjoy significant competitive benefits such as:

- *Higher profits through better customer service.* Many customers are busy and pressed for time and will pay a higher price to get faster and more convenient service. Companies that can deliver products quickly and introduce new or improved products in a timely manner will have an advantage.
- *Increased customer satisfaction.* Faster and more responsive customer service creates more satisfied customers. Companies can be more attentive to the needs of their customers and respond with more relevant product and service offerings.
- *Reduced waste and inefficiency.* Business processes in most companies can be run faster and more efficiently if they are reengineered to take advantage of new IT. These improvements can produce significant cost savings.
- *Improved management decisions.* Managers with more timely and accurate information make better decisions. Companies can reduce their risks and get better operating results with real-time data.[2]

It's All About Coordination

Those companies that are able to react quickly because of their real-time systems will have a competitive advantage. But merely reacting quickly to events is not enough. A company must also act in an appropriate and controlled manner. The proper combination of speed and control is what generates the coordination companies need. Speed without control is like stepping on the gas without being able to steer. That will only result in a crash.

Companies need to be careful not to speed up some processes without assessing the impact on other related operations. Speeding up one task only to throw other activities into confusion is counterproductive. Increased speed must be weighed against the increased costs involved. There is no point in taking speed to the level where the stability of a business process is degraded or a company's ability to control its risk is undermined.

Different areas of a company often have conflicting objectives. Inventory managers are motivated to reduce inventory. Salespeople are motivated to sell everything they can to customers. Credit people are motivated to prevent sales that could result in hard-to-collect or impossible-to-collect customer invoices. Senior management has to create complementary incentive plans for all these groups, and each group needs to understand enough about the others to effectively coordinate their interactions. This takes real effort to achieve.

Organizations need to keep several things in mind as they move into the real-time world. They should make sure that sound business strategy is what drives their efforts and not just the availability of new technology. They should redesign entire business processes before they begin applying IT. And they should set priorities so that they focus first on improving those processes that will deliver the most value to them and their customers.

A Day in the Life of an Agile Real-Time Company

To get a feel for what it is like to work in a real-time organization, let's imagine what a day in your life would be like. Last year you were promoted to Senior Vice President–North America for a large insurance company that sells insurance to businesses to cover their operating risks and related liabilities. You have put in place an ambitious plan to increase your market share in three targeted market segments. You have rolled out the plan to all your regional managers and the field sales force. People know what the big picture is and they know what their individual performance targets are within the plan. You are starting to see results that indicate the plan is working. But now is not the time to get complacent. You need to stay alert and respond effectively to events as they unfold.

The first thing you do each morning when you get to the office is open a window on the flat-screen display on your desk. The window shows a schematic diagram of operations in North America. Boxes in the diagram correspond to different parts of the business such as product sales, business operations, expenses, and revenue (see Exhibit 1.1). You call this window your dashboard because it shows you at a glance the status in key areas of your organization. The data that drives this display is updated continuously throughout the day so you can see what is happening as it occurs. This isn't a static report that is issued every month or every quarter.

This morning most of the boxes show up on the dashboard in green, indicating that actual results are tracking close to the plan. But you notice that

EXHIBIT 1.1   A SAMPLE CORPORATE DASHBOARD

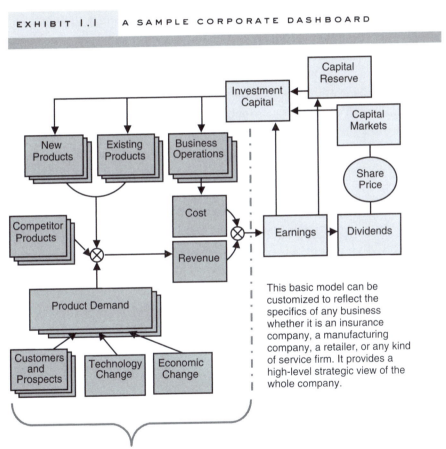

This basic model can be customized to reflect the specifics of any business whether it is an insurance company, a manufacturing company, a retailer, or any kind of service firm. It provides a high-level strategic view of the whole company.

This portion of the model can be repeated at lower and lower levels of detail for the divisional and regional organizations within a company. It provides a tactical view for division and region managers. Operating staff within these organizations have dashboards that display detail about one or more of the components of the model that relate to their jobs.

Source: Stafford Beer, *Brain of the Firm*, 2nd ed. (New York: John Wiley & Sons, Inc., 1996), p.188.

one box—revenue—is glowing yellow. "Let's see what is going on here," you think as you click on this box. It opens up to show you the key indicators you have defined to monitor activity there. Two of the indicators you defined are showing in green, but the third indicator is yellow. This indicator is the new business win ratio and you think to yourself, "We aren't selling enough new business and the trend line is not getting better. If this keeps up for another couple of months, we will never make our annual sales target."

You click on the button for the new business win ratio and up comes a geographic display of the United States and Canada and their states and provinces. Five of the regions show up in green, but one region, the North Central, shows in yellow, and another, the Northeast, shows in red. "That's Carolyn's region," you think, "I need to give her a call."

Carolyn had gotten in early that morning. She poured herself a cup of coffee and opened the dashboard window on her display screen. Carolyn's dashboard has the same layout as your dashboard, but the data it displays is only for the Northeast region. While the product sales box on your dashboard for all of North American showed up as yellow, on Carolyn's dashboard, this box glowed red. That got her attention instantly.

Clicking on the product sales box, she saw that the new business win ratio was in red. Clicking on the win ratio button, she pulled up a list showing the quotes put out last month. The list shows whether they got the business or not, and if not, the name of the company that did. What caught Carolyn's eye was the number of times a certain competitor's name showed up on that list. A company called Eat Your Lunch, Inc. was starting to win an alarming amount of new business. "I need to watch this competitor more closely," thought Carolyn. "I'm going to add an alert to my dashboard to let me know whenever Eat Your Lunch wins a bid." Carolyn then picked up the phone and began calling some of her salespeople.

Carolyn has talked to four of her top salespeople and has gotten some interesting information and a good assessment of the situation by the time you call. "I've been looking into the new business win ratio," says Carolyn. "Remember Eat Your Lunch, Inc.? We thought they were a joke. Well, it seems they have added some new features to their insurance products. They don't seem to be beating us on price, but customers love the new features. I'm going to dig into this further in the next few days. Here's what I know so far about those new features . . . ."

As you hang up, you are already formulating ideas for how to counter Eat Your Lunch's moves. You've been working with a group at headquarters to add some new features of your own to the company's policies. You thought you had more time to work out some details, but now you think, "Maybe its time to get going and roll out those new features sooner rather than later." You turn and ask your assistant to set up a session this afternoon with the task force from marketing and product development. "Tell them to run the 36-month simulations of those new features and bring the results to the meeting. Tell them to come prepared with recommendations—analysis is over. We'll be making some decisions today."

A week later, Craig, a salesman in the Northeast region, receives a set of product alerts on his dashboard. He reviews the new features that he can mix and match with existing policies to better fit customers' needs. "These are going to let me offer some very customized policies," thinks Craig. Craig taps into the client and prospect database for his territory and pulls up a list of the key people at these companies and their preferences and concerns. "I can see a number of companies whose concerns will be addressed by these new features. I'm going to contact them right away."

Along with the new feature alerts came updated pricing models. So Craig can create proposals and prices by feeding in relevant parameters like the claims history of his target companies, their operating results, and other factors. He iterates through the models several times making different assumptions and arrives at a set of proposals that he is sure his customers will find interesting.

The next morning Craig is in the office of the controller of Acme Services Company. The controller tells him that just last week a person from a company named Eat Your Lunch, Inc. was out and showed him some very innovative new insurance options. Craig showed him the updated policy he had put together and the new features that would better fit Acme's needs. Then the controller leaned forward and asked, "So what is this going to cost?"

Craig opened up his tablet PC. Through a wireless connection, he connected with his company's Web site and called up one of the new pricing models. He reviewed his assumptions with the controller to make sure he understood his needs correctly and typed some numbers into the model. Then he pressed the *calculate* button and out came a cost schedule that he handed to the controller. The controller sat back and nodded his head as he read the numbers. "We move fast," thought Craig, "We see the competition starting to make a move, and a week later the company comes out with a set of new features that are just what I need to win new business and sell more to the customers I already have."

EXECUTIVE INSIGHT

LIVING IN THE REAL-TIME WORLD

Tom Hammond is the vice president of trading operations at the Chicago Board of Trade (CBOT). Prior to this, he was the chief operating officer for the Board of Trade Clearing Corporation, and he has over 20 years of financial market experience ranging from trading to operations. Trading in stocks, commodities, and financial futures is a real-time business. Tom is an experienced executive who already operates in the kind of world that the rest of us are just now entering.

"If you look at the financial markets today," said Tom, "you see a shift in what people perceive as valuable. Execution resources [making and clearing trades] used to be what people paid for and valued. Now that's seen as a utility, and the value is in the after-market sector. It's risk management, capital management—people take these skills and apply them across many markets to do things they couldn't do before. Instead of a guy focusing on a single market like treasury bonds, he now uses his knowledge and applies it across a range of markets that interest him.

"Execution and clearing of trades used to be a mounting overhead—the more trades, the more people we needed to handle them. And at some point it becomes humanly impossible to push more volume through a trading pit even if you do add more people. Now we've made the investment to automate those activities so the more trades we handle, the better the return on our investment.

"Your highest activity levels in the past will be dwarfed by the activity to be handled in the future. If you are going to go real time, you need to make a big investment in automation, but then you have eliminated the bottlenecks and now you can handle practically unlimited volume," Tom explained. "The paradigm shift today in electronic trading hasn't been fully realized yet. Everything is automating. It is a game of distribution now. If you own the distribution, you own the world." By distribution he is referring to the number of ways CBOT can bring its trading services to customers. The more customers that use the CBOT for their trading activities, the greater are the economies of scale.

Tom's focus is shifting away from the actual execution of trades and is moving toward the issues related to building greater trading volume at the CBOT. "We've built this great automated trading system and now we are looking at ways to bring in transaction volume. I deal with questions like whether we should build our own program interfaces to customers' trading systems or whether we should just publicize the specifications for our interface and let others do that. We have decided to form partnerships with the trading system vendors and let them provide the interfaces between their systems and our trading and clearing systems. Now our distribution is not gated on what we can deliver ourselves, but instead it is gated on what our software partners can do to deliver an ever-increasing number of new customers."

Tom observed that even though they drop their trading fees to attract more volume, the trade-off is still very favorable. "Your fees drop by 50%, but your volume grows by 400%. You capture market share and you keep it because, once they are connected to your system, the switching costs are so high that customers won't leave unless you really screw up." He went on to explain that it is too costly to continue to build infrastructure to support more and more manual trading, but they can cover the cost of building systems to support automated trading as long as they keep growing their market share.

The CBOT is investing in systems to automate the bulk of its routine transactions and focusing its people on handling the nonroutine transactions or the exceptions. "The exceptions and the complex situations, that's where we want to focus our people because that is where the margins are. People will no longer pay very much for execution of routine trades," said Tom, "but there are still markets suited to face-to-face trading, what we call open-outcry trading. There are people who want a premium service and will pay a higher price to get it. You can build more complexity and subtlety into trading strategies in these markets. There is a feel that an experienced trader can develop there, and that market feel doesn't come through electronically—you have to be there in the trading pit.

"And, you know, we are also finding that the more complex the situation, the less the complexity I want in the systems I use to deal with that situation. Simple systems give me maneuverability, and in complex situations maneuverability is what I want." He pointed out that simple systems used well by experienced people are a lot more effective than complex systems that are hard to use.

When asked about things that worry him, Tom thought for a moment and then said, "It's the things you can't control, things in your distribution channels that can have a great impact on you but that are external to your company." Tom continued, "As things speed up, so does potential risk. If I can now trade 30 times a second, how many times an hour do I need to assess my risk?" Tom described how customer-facing systems are the ones that go real-time first, but they are supported by back-office systems that are not real-time. "Downstream operations after trade execution are often still batch—you can get really out of sync," he said. "You still have back-office systems that only run once a day when markets now run 22 hours a day."

"Another thing is that as you start to offer price competition, margins get very thin and you need a lot of market share to make money. I don't think there is enough market share to support 20 to 30 competitors anymore. For us, that means that our distribution becomes more and more concentrated and our risk gets more concentrated, too. You need to make sure that you and your distribution partners are strategically going in the same direction."

There is also a lot of excitement and opportunity that comes with living in a real-time world. Investments in real-time systems make it easier to enter new markets. "You can offer new products quickly and cheaply. The barriers to entering new markets are greatly reduced from even five years ago. You can sell what you are offering to an even broader range of participants. The next 10 years of my career are going to be the most exciting ones yet."

Tom has some thoughts to share with executives in other industries about operating in a real-time business world. "Regardless of where you are, don't be so satisfied or think that others using rising new technology can't unseat you. There is always someone out there willing to leverage new technology to get into a market that is too rich or to find margins that are too wide.

"The bandwidth of the Internet is going to expand dramatically," he said. "This will drive all sorts of new opportunities and launch lots of new projects to apply technology to business. These projects should be based on business need. If you can't justify a project based on clear business opportunity and good return on investment, then don't do it.

It is new, uncharted territory. Watch out that you don't forget where you are going. Use specific business needs as your compass or you will get drawn into things that become expensive research projects and deliver very little return to your business."

ENDNOTES

1. Walter Janowski, "Management Update: The Real-Time Enterprise at the Customer Front Line," *InSide Gartner:* Note Number IGG-05282003-01, 2003.
2. Ibid.

CHAPTER 2

Roots of the Real-Time Enterprise

In order to go further in our discussion about the real-time enterprise, we need to have a common foundation of ideas. I'll use a concise and powerful framework to highlight the key points, as shown in Exhibit 2.1. With an understanding of these key points you will have the concepts and vocabulary you need to both see the big picture and understand details of how a real-time enterprise works. This introduction to these concepts will give you a base of knowledge to truly understand the real-time enterprise and its implications. Concepts introduced here will be used in the following chapters to discuss ways to build and operate real-time organizations.

The real-time enterprise is not something invented in just the last few years. The principles and practices that define our thinking about the real-time enterprise have been evolving over the last 80 years or more. Important research was under way during the 1930s at organizations such as Bell Laboratories and other research labs and universities. By the late 1940s and early 1950s a series of seminal books and papers was published that introduced key theories and words. In the last 40 years continuing research and experience with actual business applications have built up a body of relevant knowledge.

This body of knowledge can be put into three broad categories labeled:

1. Scientific theory and principles
2. Techniques for measuring and managing
3. Specific business applications

EXHIBIT 2.1   ROOTS OF THE REAL-TIME ENTERPRISE

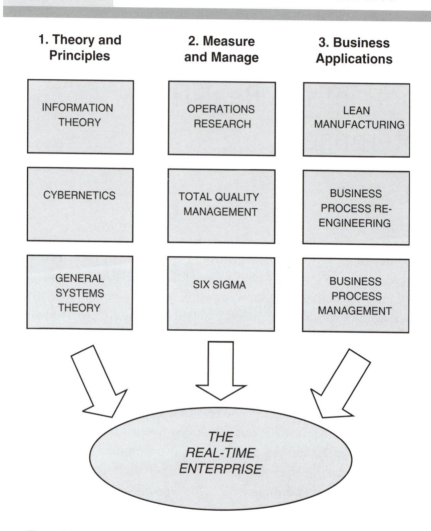

The real-time enterprise is evolving from a body of knowledge developed since the 1930s. This body of knowledge falls into three main categories: (1) scientific theory and principles; (2) techniques for measuring and managing; and (3) experience gained with specific business applications.

Let's look into each of these categories a bit further. What follows is an executive briefing on each of these categories.

SCIENTIFIC THEORY AND PRINCIPLES

There are three major theories that shape our thinking about any real-time organization or process. The first of these is *information theory*. This theory defines what information is and how information can be manipulated and transported. The second theory is *cybernetics*. Cybernetics defines ways to use information and feedback loops to control the performance of processes ranging from the operation of the autopilot on an airplane to the workings of the human nervous system. The last theory is *general systems theory*. General systems theory builds on the first two theories and goes on to define principles that describe how and why systems behave as they do.

Information Theory

In 1948 a research scientist named Claude Shannon at Bell Labs published a paper called "A Mathematical Theory of Communication" in the *Bell System Technical Journal*. Shannon's ideas form the basis for the field of information theory. They provide a way to measure the efficiency of communication systems, and they provide tools to use for solving problems associated with designing and building communication systems.

Shannon also provided a precise definition of what information is and a way to measure it. *Information* is defined as "symbols that contain unpredictable news"[1] in a white paper from Lucent Technologies. This means data that tells you something you do not already know is the real information. Data that tells you things you already know or that you can easily infer from other data is not necessary. You can drop that data from the message or substitute abbreviations for it and still communicate very clearly. For example, consider this phrase: "You dont hve 2 snd evry ltr o ech wrd 2 b undrstd."

When information is being sent from a source to a destination, you can think about it as a process containing the five steps shown in Exhibit 2.2.

The sequence of steps is:

1. The process starts with a *source* that has information to send.
2. The information is *encoded* into a message as symbols such as words, musical notes, or pictures.

EXHIBIT 2.2   FIVE-STEP INFORMATION PROCESS

Source ➝ Encoder ➝ Channel ➝ Decoder ➝ Destination

3. The message is then sent through a *channel* that has some capacity to carry information.

4. At the other end, the information is *decoded*.

5. Information is interpreted by receivers at the *destination*.

Shannon used this five-part process to present the elements of his theory and he provided a set of equations or mathematical models that describe how each element behaves within this process.

When we use Shannon's models and "do the math," we learn a lot about information and how best to transmit it. The equations tell engineers how much information can be transmitted over different kinds of communication channels. They also spell out the principles for data compression, error correction, and the amount of bandwidth needed in a channel to achieve given data transmission speeds.

When Shannon published his paper in 1948, the largest communications cable in use at that time could carry 1,800 voice conversations. Now more than 6.4 million conversations can be carried by a single strand of optical fiber that is as thin as human hair. The real-time world we are moving into demands that we be able to handle greater and greater amounts of information.

Cybernetics

The word *cybernetics* was defined in the late 1940s. In the last 20 years, however, the word has been stretched by popular culture to take on meanings that were not originally intended. The word has been sensationalized and now implies something that is futuristic and computerized and either very cool (as in *cyberspace*) or very ominous (as in *cyborgs*). This sociocultural/marketing meaning of the word is not to be confused with the way it will be used in this book. Cybernetics is a very useful word, and we will use it in the precise and rigorous manner originally intended for it.

Norbert Wiener, a professor at the Massachusetts Institute of Technology, coined the term *cybernetics* in his book by the same name.[2] He derived the word from the classical Greek word for steersman—*kybernetes*. In Wiener's words, cybernetics covers "the entire field of control and communications theory, whether in the machine or in the animal."[3] He goes on to define control as simply "the sending of messages which effectively change the behavior of the recipient."[4]

The core of cybernetic research is the discovery that the same laws govern the control and operation of any process, whether that process is mechanical, electrical, biological, economic, or social. This means that the structure and workings of any process whatsoever can be described and investigated using the same terms and relying upon the same principles.[5] Researchers and practitioners in different fields can use a common language and build upon each other's knowledge.

Central to the understanding of cybernetics are the concepts of *feedback* and *homeostasis* (see Exhibit 2.3). There are two kinds of feedback: positive and negative. Both kinds of feedback operate through the use of communication feedback loops. Homeostasis means a state of equilibrium or balance. Many processes can be seen as operating to regulate or maintain a predefined equilibrium state. Let's look at each of these concepts in a bit more detail.

Positive feedback occurs when the output of a process creates input to the process that accelerates its production of more of the same output. The effect of positive feedback is additive. It produces a result that continually builds upon itself. There is a snowballing effect. Positive feedback moves a process from one level of performance to a different level of performance. If left unchecked, positive feedback leads to the equivalent of an explosion or a collapse. Examples of positive feedback are a chain reaction in a nuclear reactor, a population explosion, or the growth of capital over time due to compound interest.

Negative feedback happens when the output of a process creates input to that process that moves the process toward a predefined goal or performance level. Negative feedback is corrective. The desired performance of a process is continually compared with its actual performance, and the resulting difference is used to take corrective action. The process adjusts its performance so as to minimize the difference between desired output and actual output. Examples of negative feedback are the operation of the cruise control in a car, which operates the car's engine to maintain a predefined speed, or the operation of a thermostat, which operates a heating unit to maintain a room's temperature at a predefined level.

EXHIBIT 2.3   FEEDBACK LOOPS

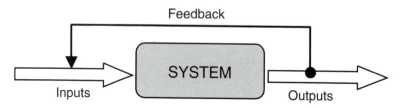

Feedback

Inputs   **SYSTEM**   Outputs

Information about the outputs that result from system actions is sent back to the system as inputs.

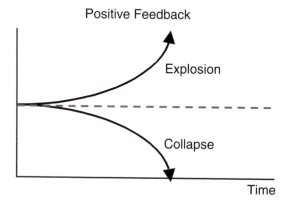

Positive Feedback

Explosion

Collapse

Time

If the feedback induces the system to continue producing more of the same output, that is positive feedback.

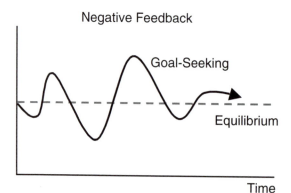

Negative Feedback

Goal-Seeking

Equilibrium

Time

If the feedback induces the system to counteract the previous output so as to seek equilibrium, that is negative feedback.

Homeostasis is defined as the point at which the process is operating at just the right level so as to be in balance with its environment or with the expectations that have been set for it. The action of negative feedback on a process constantly moves the process toward the performance level that is defined as homeostasis. The action of positive feedback on a process can result in moving the process to a new level of performance and thus a new level of homeostasis. So, it is negative feedback that maintains homeostasis and positive feedback that changes the definition of homeostasis.

General Systems Theory

During the 1950s and 1960s, people built on the insights provided by information theory and cybernetics. Two prominent researchers who established what we now call *general systems theory* or systems science are Ludwig von Bertalanffy and W. Ross Ashby. At the end of the 1960s, professor Bertalanffy published a book titled *General Systems Theory: Foundations, Development, Applications*.[6] In his book he pulled together and expanded upon material he had published in various articles and scientific papers over the previous 25 years. He noted that in surveying the evolution of modern science, a significant fact emerges. This fact is that researchers in different fields such as physics, chemistry, biology, economics, and sociology who pursued independent lines of inquiry have all wound up encountering similar problems and creating similar concepts to deal with these problems.

This led Bertalanffy to state that, "There exist models, principles, and laws that apply to generalized systems or their subclasses, irrespective of their particular kind, the nature of their component elements, and the relations or 'forces' between them." He went on to say, "In this way we postulate a new discipline called *General Systems Theory*. Its subject matter is the formulation and derivation of those principles which are valid for 'systems' in general."[7] Systems theory provides a framework that enables people to see interrelationships and patterns of change in any situation whatsoever as opposed to just analyzing static snapshots of a particular situation.

Scientists discovered that in many cases they could not explain the behavior of the whole by merely investigating the workings of each component. In their research they needed to include the way in which the parts related to or were connected with each other. This was the only way to respond to the fact that in many situations "the whole is greater than the sum of its parts." People began to conceive of the whole as an interrelated collection of components and relationships between them.

A System Definition   A system is a mental model of the world; it does not need to be an exact duplication of the "real" world. A system can be described as a set of related components and the relationships between those components. These components must interact with each other in order to accomplish a goal that is said to be the purpose of the system. System models are created to investigate and understand the workings of a particular phenomenon. Anything can be said to be a system as long as it is a collection of related components that work together to achieve a common goal.

Systems demonstrate the properties of coherence, pattern, and purpose. This means that all the components of a system are interrelated in a clearly discernable or coherent way. These interrelationships form recognizable patterns that give structure to a system. And the workings of a system are not random. It acts in a purposeful way to accomplish a goal or set of goals.

Systems are also self-regulating and persistent. Disturbances to a system from its environment will trigger interactions among the components of the system, enabling the system to recover from the effects of the disturbance and regain a state of equilibrium or homeostasis. This is what allows a system to persist over time in a changing environment. W. Ross Ashby defined this principle in formulating what he called the Law of Requisite Variety. This law states that the larger the variety of disturbances a system must cope with, the larger must be the variety of actions or responses available to the system. This law is very important when studying and designing systems that operate in high change and unpredictable environments.

General systems theory builds on information theory and cybernetics. The relationships among the components of a system are seen as being composed of information, and the information triggers either positive or negative feedback loops. The effect of these positive and negative feedback loops causes the components to act in certain ways, and this influences the behavior of the whole system.[8]

General systems theory and cybernetics are deeply intertwined and they both study essentially the same problems. To quote from *Principia Cybernetica Web* (emphasis is theirs):

> Insofar as it is meaningful to make a distinction between the two approaches, we might say that systems theory has focused more on the *struc-*

ture of systems and their models, whereas cybernetics has focused more on how systems *function*, that is to say how they control their actions, how they communicate with other systems or with their own components, . . . Since structure and function of a system cannot be understood in separation, it is clear that cybernetics and systems theory should be viewed as two facets of a single approach.[9]

These three theories—information theory, cybernetics, and general systems theory—provide the conceptual basis for discussing the dynamics and inner workings of any real-time enterprise. They enable us to understand how effective real-time systems work. We can apply these scientific principles when designing real-time organizations.

By understanding these basic theories, you give yourself a firm foundation upon which to participate in the lively debate about how to best build real-time organizations and how they will change our economy. Now let's look at a set of techniques that we can use to manage the operations of any real-time enterprise.

TECHNIQUES FOR MEASURING AND MANAGING

Over the last 60 years a number of techniques have evolved to help organizations measure and manage their operations. We will take a look here at three of the most influential techniques: operations research (OR), total quality management (TQM), and six sigma (6σ). These are the techniques that enable people to effectively operate a real-time enterprise.

Operations Research

Operations research (OR) got its start during World War II as a response to the urgent need to solve problems that ranged from finding the best way to organize production in a factory to designing the best search patterns for detecting enemy submarines. OR is also known as management science and is a scientific approach to analyzing problems and making decisions. People trained in OR analyze problems and break them down into components that can be solved mathematically using various equations and mathematical models. Once the problem components have been defined by mathematical models, computer simulation is used to forecast the effects of different choices and identify the best alternatives.

Operations research can address a whole range of problems faced by businesses, governments, and other organizations. These problems typically involve designing workflow processes that will operate in the most efficient manner or deciding how to apply scarce resources such as people, facilities, and money to get the best results. For example, have you ever noticed that some companies (like Walt Disney World) do a great job of managing long lines at popular exhibits and rides? That's because they use an OR technique called *queuing theory* that shows how to deal with flows of people or goods in the most efficient manner.

In addition to queuing theory, there is a collection of other techniques that OR can bring to bear on a problem. Key techniques include:

- *Critical path method (CPM) or project evaluation and review technique (PERT).* Offers methods for dealing with many inter-related tasks that must be effectively coordinated. It answers questions about which tasks in a project must come before and which must come after another task and which tasks can occur simultaneously.

- *Linear programming.* Involves the allocation of scarce resources among competing alternatives in order to achieve some objective. This technique will answer questions such as how best to allocate a fixed advertising budget across various media or how to schedule production using available factories to best meet forecasted demand for different products.

- *Network modeling.* Used to analyze situations that can be conceptualized as a network. This applies to situations such as the flow of messages through a communication system or the flow of traffic through city streets. Network modeling can provide answers for how to maximize message flow through a network or minimize travel time from one point to another on a network.

Total Quality Management

Total quality management (TQM) is the second technique. W. Edwards Deming is credited with articulating many of the practices in this area. He spent over 50 years developing these practices and applying and teaching them in factories in Japan and the United States. People such as W. Edwards Deming, Dr. Kaoru Ishikawa, and Philip B. Crosby defined and popularized many of the tools and processes used in TQM. TQM emphasizes that quality is a culture that develops in an organization. First, company management embraces it and then it spreads to all the people that work there. One of the most notable features of TQM is the use of quality circles composed of employees who have been trained in problem solving and quality control techniques.

The tools of quality control are taught to all employees so that they can use them to improve operations in different parts of the business. Some of these tools are:

- *Cause-and-effect diagrams.* Also known as fishbone diagrams because they use a structure that looks like the skeleton of a fish. These diagrams are used to help a quality team brainstorm possible causes of a problem.

- *Check sheets.* The forms used to collect and organize data. Computer spreadsheets are often used as check sheets. Check sheets are designed so as to capture the right data about a situation and also to make the data gathering as easy as possible.

- *Pareto charts.* Bar charts that show the frequency distribution of discrete data points or events. They are useful when trying to find out which category of events has the greatest impact on a situation.

- *Histograms.* Another type of bar chart that shows the distribution or variations of certain variables within a body of data. For instance, a histogram can show the frequency by age group of customers who buy classical music or red sports cars.

- *Scatter diagrams.* Graphs that help people look for a direct relationship between any two factors in an operation. For instance, to understand the relationship between the number of order takers and average customer wait time, data reflecting these two values can be plotted and analyzed.

- *Trend charts.* Graphs that show how things are changing over time. This graph shows the performance trends of a single index or group of indices such as days sales outstanding, inventory turns, number of late deliveries, weekly sales, and so on. Examples of these tools are shown in Exhibit 2.4.

Six Sigma

The third technique is six sigma (6σ). This technique builds on TQM and takes the definition of quality to a new level. Six sigma started at Motorola

EXHIBIT 2.4 TOOLS FOR QUALITY CONTROL

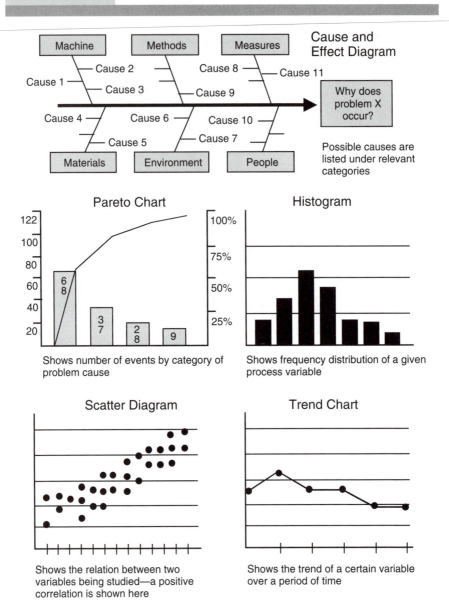

Cause and Effect Diagram

Machine | Methods | Measures

Cause 2 — Cause 8 — Cause 11
Cause 1 — Cause 3 — Cause 9

Why does problem X occur?

Cause 4 — Cause 6 — Cause 10
Cause 5 — Cause 7

Materials | Environment | People

Possible causes are listed under relevant categories

Pareto Chart

Shows number of events by category of problem cause

Histogram

Shows frequency distribution of a given process variable

Scatter Diagram

Shows the relation between two variables being studied—a positive correlation is shown here

Trend Chart

Shows the trend of a certain variable over a period of time

in the 1980s and over the last 20 years has spread to many other organizations. Six sigma is a statistical measure of the performance of a process or the quality of a product. A process operating at a 6σ level produces less than 3.4 defects or errors per million opportunities. Six sigma is a clear definition of excellence that all organizations can aim for. It provides a common measure for performance across different processes and products, and it can be used to compare, discuss, and learn from different operations in different parts of a company.

To get a sigma measurement for a process, a company first defines the customer that the process serves and then defines what that customer expects from the process. Data is collected and graphed as a histogram or a bell curve showing the frequency distribution of the process outcome. The graph shows how many times the outcome met customer expectations and how many times it did not.

One sigma means the process met customer expectations 30.9% of the time. Two sigma means 69.1%, three sigma means 93.3%, four sigma means 99.4%, five sigma is 99.97%, and six sigma is 99.99966%. Most companies operate in the range between two and three sigma. A 93.3% percent customer satisfaction rate (3σ) is good, but it means that there are still 66,807 failures per million events. That can produce a lot of unhappy customers and unnecessary expense.

In addition to being a universal performance measurement, 6σ is also a process that guides companies and project teams through the activities needed to improve their operations and their products. These activities are encompassed in a five-step process: (1) define, (2) measure, (3) analyze, (4) improve, and (5) control.[10] The process is known as DMAIC (first letter of each step), pronounced "dee-MAY-ic." Let's take a look at the activities in each step. See Exhibit 2.5.

Define   This step begins every 6σ project. There are three important documents produced in this step. The first document is the project charter. The charter lays out the business case and the problem statement. It also clearly defines the project scope so that the project team knows exactly what they should focus on and what areas they should not get into. The charter goes on to state the goal or mission of the project and the specific objectives that the team needs to achieve in order to accomplish the goal. Milestones are laid out that indicate to the team where they should be in the DMAIC process

EXHIBIT 2.5   FIVE STEPS IN THE SIX SIGMA PROCESS

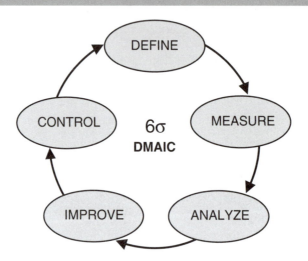

A six sigma team goes through these five steps as they identify the problem, gather relevant data, and devise and implement a process improvement.

by what dates. Finally, the charter describes the roles and responsibilities of the team members, the team leader, and the project executive sponsor.

In addition to the project charter, this step also defines and documents the customers that will be served and their needs and expectations. The needs and expectations of the customers tell the team what to measure and improve. The third document produced is a high-level process map that shows the tasks involved in the process and the inputs and outputs of each task. The high-level process map shows everyone involved with the project the exact sequence of tasks that will be candidates for improvement.

Measure   In this step the project team creates a data collection plan and then goes and collects data that measures the current state of the process or product that they are going to improve. The data to be collected is based on the customer requirements and will show how often the process meets customer requirements. The data will also show the activity levels of key tasks in the process.

The team then goes and collects the data and calculates the existing sigma measurement for the process. This obvious step of collecting data and documenting the current situation is often overlooked or done poorly because the project team thinks they already know what is wrong and they want to get on to the step of fixing the problem. Doing good data collection goes a long way toward getting the project off to a start in the right direction.

Analyze   At this point the project team applies statistical tools to discover and validate root causes of problems. Many of the tools used in this step come from TQM. The team uses cause-and-effect diagrams and frequency distribution charts to pinpoint the sources of error in the process being investigated. They use scatter diagrams to test the strength of correlations between one variable and another in the process. They use run charts to track the performance patterns of various tasks and of the process overall.

As the problems are pinpointed, the team then formulates options for eliminating or reducing these problems. They compare the different options with each other. How difficult is each option? How much will each one cost? What impact will each option have on improving the sigma measure of the process?

Improve   In this step the team leader works with the project's executive sponsor to select a group of improvement options. The options with the best chance for success and with the greatest impact on the process are the ones to choose.

With the sponsor's backing, the 6σ team implements the selected improvements to the process. Best practice calls for the team to implement the improvements one at a time or in small groups of related improvements. After implementing each improvement, the team should collect process performance data and recalculate the sigma measure—hopefully, the sigma measure is going up. This ensures that either the improvements actually provide valuable results or they are discontinued.

Control   Once improvements have been made to a process, there needs to be a way to regularly monitor it to see that the improvements stay in place and remain effective. The 6σ project team defines a set of measurements that will be collected on an ongoing basis to document performance levels of the improved process.

In addition, the team creates a response plan that lays out what corrective action to take if ongoing performance measures indicate that the improvements are beginning to slip. Over the longer term, the greatest benefit from the 6σ approach is that organizations reap the very real benefits of process improvements that continue to improve and thus deliver more and more value. (See Exhibit 2.6.)

These three techniques—OR, TQM, and 6σ—are the tools we need in order to operate a real-time enterprise. They provide ways to continually monitor what is happening, spot problems and opportunities, and take effective action to get the results we want. The skillful application of these

EXHIBIT 2.6   SIX SIGMA (6σ) PERFORMANCE IS ALMOST PERFECT

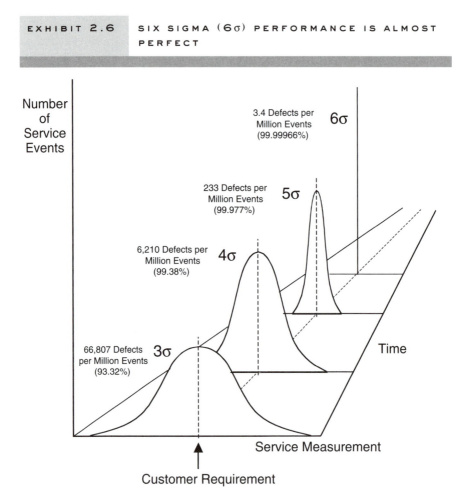

Most business processes operate at between 2σ and 3σ. This means they produce between 308,500 and 66,807 defects per million events. That equates to a lot of dissatisfied customers. Competitive advantage goes to those companies that can drive their performance levels closest to 6σ and then keep it there.

techniques by people in a real-time organization is what will enable the organization as a whole to achieve the high levels of performance that a real-time enterprise can achieve.

SPECIFIC BUSINESS APPLICATIONS

As a response to changing economic conditions, businesses have been experimenting with ways to apply the theories and techniques described in the previous two sections. It has been a learning process for everyone. Three of the most influential applications are *lean manufacturing, business process reengineering,* and *business process management.* As companies begin to incorporate these applications into their mode of operations, they are becoming real-time enterprises. These are the applications that make real time happen in a company.

Lean Manufacturing

In the 1960s and 1970s Toyota's car-making plants were implementing and reaping great benefits from a particular approach to manufacturing that they called the Toyota Production System (also known as *just-in-time* or *JIT manufacturing*). The purpose of this system was to streamline the production process to eliminate waste in time and material and improve quality. The whole production process was designed so as to eliminate steps that did not directly add value to the products being manufactured.

Toyota recognized that the market itself set car prices and that no single company could increase those prices and still remain competitive. Therefore, Toyota created a system in which the overall goal was to increase profits by decreasing costs. They created a system that used far less factory space and inventory and that greatly shortened product development times as compared to competitors using traditional mass production methods. Their system also reduced product defects and increased product variety. Toyota and other Japanese car manufacturers used the combination of lower costs and higher quality to deliver more value to customers. They achieved market dominance through superior manufacturing systems, not through marketing and sales campaigns.

The Toyota system spread throughout the manufacturing industry in the 1980s and 1990s. Its principles have been generalized and further developed, and the system is now referred to as *lean manufacturing*. Some key concepts of lean manufacturing are:[11]

- *Eliminate non-value-added steps* in the production and delivery of products or services that do things the end use customer is not willing to pay for.

- *Eliminate wait times* in processes in which component parts or finished goods accumulate and wait to be used.

- *Use appropriately sized machines* that can be quickly changed over to efficiently produce varying quantities of many different parts.

- *Position these machines in production sequences* that can quickly respond to actual customer demands for specific products.

- *Refine production sequences* so that the number of steps, the amount of time, and the manufacturing complexity required to serve the customer continually decrease.

Lean manufacturing methods are gradually replacing the older mass production methods. Lean manufacturing uses a strategy focused on the needs of the customer and on identifying and exploiting new competitive opportunities as customer needs change. Mass production focuses on achieving economies of scale using standardized technologies and a few stable product designs. Lean companies use flat organization structures that encourage initiative and innovation and efficient information flows throughout the company. Mass production companies use hierarchical organization structures that encourage people to just follow orders and stay with traditional procedures. Information filters only slowly through predefined channels in these companies.

Mass production companies focus on maximizing return on individual assets by running big machines fast for long periods of time to absorb labor and overhead. Lean manufacturing companies look at the entire production process using a systems perspective. They seek to reduce overall costs and maximize customer value and responsiveness by managing the entire process rather than optimizing the usage of individual machines.

Business Process Reengineering

Michael Hammer and James Champy wrote a book in 1993 titled, *Reengineering the Corporation: A Manifesto for Business*.[12] It ushered in a business practice known as business process reengineering (BPR). BPR was launched as a way to jump-start the transformation from hierarchical, mass production–oriented companies to companies that were more flexible, more cost efficient, and more responsive to customer needs and changing markets.

Companies needed to move beyond being organized as functional departments such as sales, purchasing, manufacturing, and accounting all operating under a bureaucratic command-and-control structure. This had been the norm for the previous 80 years, and something dramatic was needed to break old ways of thinking. In their book, Hammer and Champy defined business process reengineering as "The fundamental rethinking and radical redesign of business processes to bring about dramatic improvements in critical, contemporary measures of performance, such as cost, quality, service, and speed."[13]

As well as reducing costs, reengineering also aims to increase a company's responsiveness to change and its ability to capitalize on new market developments. To do this, the reengineering process calls for a company to work through some basic steps over a set period of time (often three to nine months).

Strategic Planning   This is the first step. The strategic plan defines the company's vision or reason for being and the goals that the company needs to realize in order to live up to its vision. It goes on to describe the markets it serves and the opportunities that those markets present. The plan lays out how the company will use the resources and skills available to it to exploit market opportunities and reach its goals. Once the strategic plan is done, it may stay in place for several years while the company iterates through the steps shown below.

Business or Operations Planning   The next step is to identify the business objectives and performance measurements that need to be achieved to reach company goals. The business plan defines the exact output of products and services that the company must produce to meet customer demands. It also describes the information systems requirements needed to support the delivery of these products and services.

Process Mapping   This technique is used to map out the activities that make up a business process. Process mapping documents the inputs required by each activity and the outputs created by each activity. It also describes how each activity transforms its inputs into outputs. Process maps are used to illustrate and document existing processes and proposed new processes.

Data Modeling   This is a technique for describing the data used by all the activities in a business process. The data model defines the things or entities about which data must be collected. For each data entity, it defines the kinds of data or data attributes that need to be known. For instance, for an entity called customer, some data attributes would be name, address, credit limit, and so on.

Activity-Based Costing (ABC)   ABC is a technique that is an extension of process mapping. It allows people to calculate the costs of each activity in a process and for the entire business processes. ABC can measure the costs of the processes that produce the basic goods and services provided by a company.

Process Design   In this step people either redesign existing processes or design entirely new business processes for production and delivery of the company's goods and services. People use process maps and ABC to evaluate different processes. They investigate how other companies in similar situations have designed their processes (known as *best practices*). The process design documents the new activity sequences and the information, staff, and other resources needed to implement a new business processes.

Process Implementation   This is where the new process designs get built. This step involves the restructuring of the company's organization and the installation of new information systems. People are trained in new activities and procedures and their pay and bonus incentives are changed to support the new ways of doing things.

Business Process Management

Change requires a lot of effort, so companies doing reengineering often tend to emphasize a one-time, big bang approach to changing things. Sometimes big changes are successfully made. Other times only partial changes are made, and after a while the situation settles back into the old ways of doing things that had existed previously.

Business process management (BPM) has come about as a response to this problem. It is a way for an organization to carry out a continuous, incremental process of improving operational performance. Related to BPM is a set of supporting applications called business activity monitoring (BAM) that provide a constant flow of up-to-the-minute data about operations within a company and between it and its trading partners. Companies have enormous opportunities to cut costs and generate new sources of revenue if they can improve the operations of certain key processes.

Howard Smith and Peter Fingar state in their book, *Business Process Management: The Third Wave,* that, "BPM is therefore the convergence of management theory—total quality management, Six Sigma, business engineering, and general systems thinking—with modern technologies. . . ."[14] BPM uses an intuitive graphical notation to draw and describe process maps. This graphical notation provides a common language that allows both businesspeople and technical people to work together effectively to design and operate business processes.

In a lean and responsive organization, business processes must manage themselves as much as possible and not rely on a centralized command-and-control system. Cybernetics and general systems theory show us ways to design such processes. By using information flows and negative feedback loops, a company can design and implement processes that continuously correct their behavior in order to steer toward predefined performance targets. In this way, self-managing processes amplify the productivity of employees as well as reduce defects and increase quality.

Business process management gives companies a way to focus on their core competencies and outsource processes that do not give them any competitive advantages or useful differentiation in the eyes of their customers. Companies start by using a process-mapping method to define their business processes. There are a number of different process-mapping methods. Two of the more popular methods are IDEF0 and BPMN. IDEF0 (Integrated Definition Level 0) is a public domain modeling system created by the U.S. Air Force. BPMN (Business Process Modeling Notation) is a creation of the Business Process Management Initiative (BPMI.org). Once the data and the task logic for the activities in a particular process have been described, the decision can be made to either perform the process in-house or to outsource it. Companies need to focus on particular processes wherein they add unique value and outsource other processes to service providers who can perform them more efficiently.

The control and coordination that BPM makes possible within and between companies will drive the creation of new organizational models. The Internet and other communications networks make it easy and cost effective for companies to electronically connect to each other. These electronic connections blur the boundaries between companies. They open up opportunities to outsource processes, yet still have the ability to coordinate closely with the people doing that work. Companies can then shift their energies and attention toward doing the value-added things their customers pay them for and exploring for new opportunities.

Lean manufacturing, BPR, and BPM are creating the kind of organization that we call the real-time enterprise. It is the use of these applications that enables an organization to continuously monitor and adjust to its changing environment. The success companies are having with these applications is causing them to experiment with new kinds of organizational structures. In Chapter 3, we will look in more detail at the kinds of organizational structures that best support a real-time enterprise.

THOUGHT LEADER INTERVIEW

INCREASING RETURNS AND THE MODERN ECONOMY

W. Brian Arthur is an external professor and former director of the Economics Research Program at the Santa Fe Institute. He won the Schumpeter Prize in Economics in 1990 and was Morrison Professor of Economics and Population Studies at Stanford University from 1983 to 1996. He has a PhD in operations research from the University of California at Berkeley and an MA in mathematics from University of Michigan at Ann Arbor.

Brian Arthur has done research in three areas of interest. The first area is the phenomenon of increasing returns. He is studying the dynamics of market lock-in in which one out of a group of contenders goes on to achieve almost complete dominance of a market. The second area is cognition and economics. This involves investigation of how people "cognize" problems and how they operate in ambiguous or indeterminate situations. Most recently, he is researching how technology and the modern economy evolve together. He is looking at how technology changes and the impact this has on our economy. These areas overlap one another, and together they create a framework that is very useful for discussing the new real-time world that is growing up around us.

"The traditional economy I learned about in university was a Victorian economy where process-oriented companies performed activities such as coal mining, making steel, or manufacturing cars. In those processes, one eventually runs into the law of diminishing returns, and this has a balancing effect on the size of any company in that economy." But now, Brian observed, "products are becoming lighter—they are more information than they are stuff. The costs in the high-tech economy are lots of up-front R&D [research and development] to create the first copy, and then every copy of the product after that costs almost nothing. There is no point of diminishing returns; instead, there are increasing returns—operating costs as a percentage of units sold decrease instead of increase."

This creates extremely competitive situations because the stakes are so high. The R&D to develop a product is often very expensive but the potential return is enormous. If a company can pull out ahead in a market and get a critical mass of people to use its product, then it stands to lock in and own that market. "Increasing returns is another name for positive feedback," said Brian. Economies driven by positive feedback are increasingly the norm, and these economies are what can be called "winner-take-all" economies. "The hypercompetitive economy is already here."

Brian went on to point out that, "The more high-tech a business gets, the more it becomes a cognitive business. Old-style businesses were largely composed of repetitive processes. New business is usually not a repeated process. Every problem is a fresh new problem." Markets evolve, new competitors enter, and it isn't clear what they will do. Brian describes these situations as being "all about cognition. The skill is to figure out what the game is. You are in a game without knowing what the rules are. You have to make important decisions up front before your new product is fully developed. You don't know how well it will work or what your competitors will do. You are caught up in the fog of technology.

"The job for the CEO is to frame up the problem. Bill Gates, for instance, is excellent at figuring out when the rules change. He made a gestalt shift from playing a shrink-wrapped software game to playing a web game. The companies that get blind-sided are the ones that don't know what the game is." Brian explained that people who are focused on product in a high-tech world do not do well because they concentrate on manufacturing efficiency and quality control instead of responding to new market demands. "Strategy—the timing, how to get into a market, where to enter—is much more important than operating decisions."

"In high tech you need to observe, observe, observe. You need to keep your finger on the pulse of what's happening this week. You want your techie types to be closer to the market, not hidden away in a lab or an office. Glean ideas from conferences, think about how they apply to your company's products and services." Today's high-tech products are evolving combinations of features and functions. It is critical to know what functions your markets value now and what game is being played now.

When asked about how he sees the impact of technology on our economy, Brian responded, "What's going on is a massive interconnection of business processes. Companies need to ask what functions they can provide themselves and what functions can they acquire from other companies. Information technology is providing a neural system for the economy and this is producing a huge increase in productivity. In the same sense that railroad networks connect places, information technology networks connect processes.

"This is all having a profound impact on the meaning of work," said Brian. "For most primitive people their life was harsh but they were not that busy all the time. They spent time waiting for opportunities, for seasons to change." He described how the industrial revolution came along and work was defined as the long hours people spent doing repetitious tasks. Now the information economy is here and "we are being released from work of a repetitious nature but we still don't want to be released into indolence. We want to work but what is the definition of work now?"

ENDNOTES

1. Lucent Technologies, "Bell Labs Celebrates 50 Years of Information Theory," (Murray Hill, NJ: Lucent Technologies), *http://www.lucent.com/*.

2. Norbert Wiener, *Cybernetics* (Cambridge, MA: Massachusetts Institute of Technology Press, 1948).

3. Ibid., p. 11.

4. Ibid., p. 12.

5. A book that examines the impact of cybernetics on society is also written by Norbert Wiener, *The Human Use of Human Beings: Cybernetics and Society* (Boston, MA: Houghton Mifflin Company, 1950).

6. Ludwig von Bertalanffy, *General Systems Theory: Foundations, Development, Applications* (Middlesex, England: Penguin Books, 1968).

7. Ibid.
8. Another very thoughtful and insightful book on systems theory is written by Ervin Laszlo, *Introduction to Systems Philosophy: Toward a New Paradigm of Contemporary Thought* (New York: Harper & Row, 1972).
9. F. Heylighen, "Cybernetics and Systems Theory," in F. Heylighen, C. Joslyn, and V. Turchin (eds.), *Principia Cybernetica Web* (Brussels: Principia Cybernetica, 2000), *http://pespmc1.vub.ac.be/REFERPCP.html*.
10. George Eckes, *Six Sigma for Everyone* (New York: John Wiley & Sons, Inc., 2003), p. 29.
11. Michael L. George, *Lean Six Sigma: Combining Six Sigma Quality with Lean Speed* (New York: McGraw-Hill, 2002), p. 35.
12. James Champy and Michael Hammer, *Reengineering the Corporation: A Manifesto for Business Revolution* (New York: HarperCollins, 1993).
13. Ibid.
14. Peter Fingar and Howard Smith, *Business Process Management: The Third Wave* (Tampa, FL: Meghan-Kiffer Press, 2003), p. 73.

CHAPTER 3

Structure of Real-Time Organizations

For the last 200 years most organizations have employed versions of the hierarchical organization structure. This kind of structure served us well in a world where information moved only periodically and where change was not as fast or as prevalent as it is today. The pyramid-shaped hierarchy is a classical and archetypal organization structure. It is the structure most commonly used in organizations everywhere, from multinational corporations to governments and the military.

Up until the mid-twentieth century, the means to capture and move information consisted largely of words and numbers written or printed on paper that was then physically transported from one place to another. From the perspective of information theory, that is a channel with a very slow data transmission rate. Even with the introduction of the telegraph and the telephone, the overall speed of data transmission within most organizations remained slow.

In a world where information moves slowly, a centrally directed hierarchy is a good way to organize. It allows managers to control the operations of large numbers of people and machines. Plans are made, orders are given, and people simply do as they are told. Such an organization can respond only slowly to changes in its environment, and it takes a while to even see a change. This is because data is filtered and summarized as it gets collected and passed back through channels to the decision makers. But if the means do not exist to quickly handle lots of data anyway, this slowness is not so bad compared to the benefits that a hierarchy offers.

However, in the last 20 years, computing and communications technology have made it possible for organizations of any size to quickly collect, transmit, and analyze enormous amounts of data. That means it is now possible to respond to change much faster. It is possible to operate more efficiently and reap greater profits from opportunities that arise.

This changes the results of the calculation when we evaluate the costs and benefits of the traditional hierarchical organization structure. Using applications like lean manufacturing, business process reengineering (BPR), and business process management (BPM), companies can adopt new and more efficient organizational structures.

There are four theories that give us a vocabulary of ideas and techniques so that we can talk about designing real-time organizational structures. Let's look at these concepts in a bit more detail. These key concepts are:

1. Complex adaptive systems
2. System dynamics
3. The viable systems model
4. The soft systems model

COMPLEX ADAPTIVE SYSTEMS

The real world is a complex place. There is a lot going on and lots of interrelationships among the things that are happening. Sometimes events and the relationships between them are obvious, and other times the relationships are very subtle. Classical hierarchies are blind to this complexity. They deal with complexity by simply filtering most of it out. Companies that can better see and respond to the complexities of their world are clearly going to have big competitive advantages over those that cannot. These are the companies we are starting to refer to as *real-time enterprises*.

So what do these companies look like? How are they organized? How do they operate? Some answers to such questions can be found by studying what are known as *complex adaptive systems* (CASs). General systems theory and cybernetics give us tools to investigate and describe the workings of such systems. A CAS is a system that can change its behavior in response to its environment so as to either accomplish a new goal or maintain its existing homeostasis (internal equilibrium). Such a system uses positive and negative feedback from its environment and from its internal operations to guide its behavior.

Our thinking about CASs is shaped by a group of people who have studied the subject over the last several decades. Let's take a closer look at four prominent people in this group: Jay Forrester, Stafford Beer, Peter Checkland, and Peter Senge.

Jay Forrester has explored systems behavior since the late 1950s. During much of this time he was a professor of management at the Massachusetts Institute of Technology (MIT), Sloan School of Management. There, he applied his background in computer sciences and engineering to the development of computer modeling and analysis of social systems leading to a field now known as *system dynamics*.[1] He developed the field of system dynamics as a way to assess how different policies and courses of action will affect growth, stability, fluctuation, and changing behavior in corporations, cities, and countries.

Stafford Beer explored the application of cybernetic principles to business and their effect on the design of business organizations. He founded two pioneering and well-respected operations research (OR) societies, and he was a leader in the development of systems ideas. He was a consultant to companies and governments worldwide and was a lecturer at universities in Europe and America. He is widely recognized as the founder of management cybernetics, which he defined as "the science of effective organization."[2] He built on the work of Norbert Weiner and W. Ross Ashby and synthesized many of his ideas into what is known as the *viable systems model* (VSM).

Peter Checkland began his career as a manager of research and development for 15 years at a large British industrial corporation. He is now a professor of systems at Lancaster University, Lancaster, United Kingdom. His research focuses on systems thinking and its relation to real-world problem solving, especially as it relates to the creation of information systems.[3] His work led to the development of the soft systems methodology (SSM) as a systemic process of inquiry into the workings of business, social, and governmental systems.

Peter Senge is a senior lecturer at MIT. He is also the founding chairperson of the Society for Organizational Learning (SoL). SoL is a global organization composed of corporations, researchers, and consultants dedicated to the "interdependent development of people and their institutions."[4] His areas of special interest focus on decentralizing the role of leadership and control in organizations so as to enhance people's capacity to work cooperatively and effectively toward common goals. He is the author of the book *The Fifth Discipline: The Art and Practice of the Learning Organization.*[5] This book builds upon the soft systems methodology of Peter Checkland, and it has popularized systems thinking in many organizations since the 1990s.

System Dynamics

Jay Forrester explained a phenomenon that many of us have observed. He pointed out that complex systems require homeostasis in order to maintain stability and to survive. So their entire structural and functional organization is oriented to the maintenance of their internal status quo. This leads them to behave in ways that are counterintuitive. When you expect them to react in a certain way to a specific action, complex systems instead do something completely unexpected and seemingly contrary to common sense. Businesspeople, politicians, and social scientists know this behavior only too well.

Quite often, what happens is that policies and actions designed to address a problem wind up making the problem worse instead of better. Forrester explained that a complex system such as a corporation, a city, or an economy behaves in ways that are quite the opposite of the way a simple system behaves.

Our expectations of complex systems are not accurate because most of our intuitive understanding of systems has been shaped by experience with simple systems. The behavior of simple systems is driven by what is known as first-order, negative-feedback loops. These systems are goal-seeking systems that have only one important variable to control. Take, for example, the workings of a thermostat. If the room is too hot, we turn down the thermostat. If the temperature is too low, we turn up the thermostat. Or consider regulating the speed of your car. If the speed is too slow, you step on the accelerator; if the speed is too fast, you take your foot off the accelerator.

The simple feedback loops that govern the workings of these systems condition us to expect to see cause and effect occur at the same time and in the same place. Our problems in dealing with complex systems arise because in these systems cause and effect usually are not closely related in either time or place. There are many feedback loops in operation. Some of these are positive-feedback loops and others are negative-feedback loops. It is the interplay of all these feedback loops that determines the system's response and not just the action of any single feedback loop. The behavior of the system is determined by its overall structure and the operating policies that govern the relationships among its component parts.

Our problems with complex systems are then compounded by the fact that since we expect to see cause and effect closely related in time and place, we tend to see cause-and-effect relationships where in fact none exist. We see an apparent cause for something that in reality is only a coincidental effect. Cause-and-effect associations are made between variables that are not directly related but that exhibit an apparent action–reaction response because they are moving together as part of the overall dynamics of the system. We miss root causes and wind up treating coincident symptoms—and the results range from ineffectual to downright harmful.

Forrester also investigated and explained two other characteristics of CASs (see Exhibit 3.1). The first of these is that there is often a conflict between the short-term and long-term consequences of a change in policy or operating procedures. Policies that produce short-term benefits often create long-term problems, and policies that create long-term improvements usually create negative consequences in the short term. The other characteristic is that there is almost always a conflict between the goals of an individual subsystem and the well-being of the total system. There is a constant struggle between subsystems trying to optimize their performance and the broader system that is trying to maximize the overall system performance.[6]

EXHIBIT 3.1   CHARACTERISTICS OF COMPLEX SYSTEMS

1. Behavior of complex systems tends to be counterintuitive.

2. Cause and effect in complex systems are usually not closely related in time and place, yet we mistakenly see cause-and-effect relationships where none exist because our experience with simple systems leads us to do so.

3. It is common to miss root causes and focus instead on coincidental symptoms that seem related because they occur closely in time and place.

4. System changes that produce short-term improvements often lead to long-term problems, and changes that produce long-term benefits often create short-term problems.

5. There is usually a conflict between optimizing the performance of any one subsystem and maximizing the well-being of the entire system.

Viable Systems Model

Stafford Beer's studies led him to view the human body as a model for describing what a complex system should look like in order to be successful. He named this model the viable systems model. The VSM looks at an organization as if it were a living thing and describes how the organization should be structured. Stafford Beer published two books—*Brain of the Firm* and *The Heart of Enterprise*—that explained the VSM.[7]

The VSM views a situation as being composed of three components: (1) the environment; (2) the operations performed by a system in this environment; and (3) the metasystem activities of coordination, planning, and goal setting done by a system in this environment.

Next, the model identifies five basic subsystems that form the operations and metasystem components of any system. The basic subsystems are referred to as systems 1, 2, 3, 4, and 5. Let's take a closer look at what each of these systems does.

System 1 is the collection of operating units that carry out the primary activities of the organization. System 1 is composed of all the units that actually do something. This is analogous to the muscles and organs in the human body.

System 2 is like the autonomic nervous system that monitors the interactions of the muscles and organs. This is the system that has responsibility for resolving conflicts among operating units and for maintaining stability.

System 3 is the system that looks across the entire body of muscles and organs and optimizes their collective operations for the benefit of the whole body. This system also performs functions that are analogous to those of the autonomic nervous system. In addition, system 3 is responsible for finding ways to generate synergies among operating units.

System 4 is like our conscious nervous system. It looks out at the environment, collects information, and makes predictions and forecasts about the environment. It also picks strategies and makes plans for best adapting to the environment.

System 5 is analogous to our higher brain functions. It defines the system's identity and its overall vision or reason for being. This system decides on operating policies and guidelines that the system will follow. (See Exhibit 3.2.)

The model states that in order for a system to be a viable system it must be able to create, implement, and regulate its own operating policies. This

EXHIBIT 3.2   THE VIABLE SYSTEMS MODEL

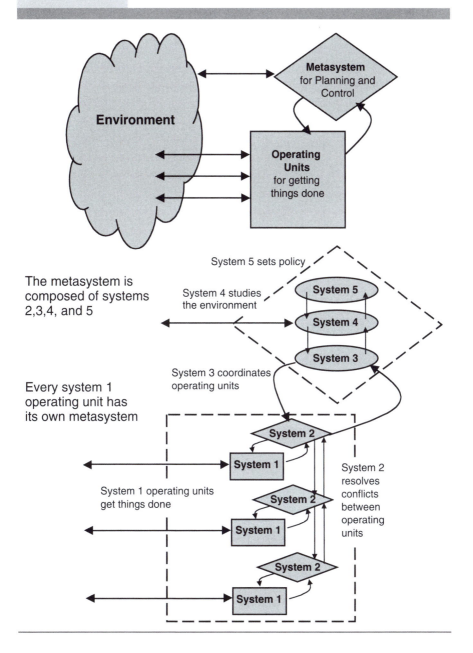

means a viable system needs to have the five systems described above. If a system cannot create, implement, and regulate its own policies, then it is a component part of some other system. Such a system all by itself would not have the ability to sustain itself over time.

The model also emphasizes that the individual operating units (the system 1 of an organization) need to be as autonomous as possible. They need to be free to devise and execute their own operations within predefined performance ranges and areas of responsibility. Each operating unit within system 1 is actually a microcosm of the entire system. Each operating unit contains its own systems 1 through 5.

Because each operating unit in system 1 is autonomous and self-regulating, their activities are not directly controlled by systems 2 and 3, but instead they are coordinated through the action of feedback that occurs among systems 1, 2, and 3. Systems 2 and 3 monitor data generated by system 1 and look for changes in status or for indications that an operating unit has gone outside of its agreed-upon performance range.

When they see a status change or an out-of-range condition, systems 2 and 3 send this information back to system 1. This sets up either a positive- or negative-feedback loop that guides the activities of the individual operating units. Response by an operating unit to feedback from system 2 or 3 allows it to regulate its own behavior and respond as needed.

Response to feedback is not to be confused with following an order. System 2 or 3 does not send an order to system 1 to do something. Instead, the guiding effect produced by feedback among the systems is used as an alternative to command authority. This enables each operating unit to act autonomously. This autonomy allows each unit to think and act for itself as long as it stays within agreed-upon limits. The system as a whole then benefits from the initiative and responsiveness displayed by the autonomous operating units. In addition, systems 2 and 3 are not bogged down trying to do the thinking for system 1, so they do a better job of monitoring and maximizing overall system performance.

Soft Systems Model

In 1981 Peter Checkland published a book titled *Systems Thinking, Systems Practice*.[8] In this book he makes the argument that conceptualizing the world as a system of interrelated processes is a useful method for understanding those processes. He goes on to state that the approaches used to analyze "hard" systems such as electronic or software systems or mechanical systems is not suitable for analyzing "soft" systems. Soft systems are systems that involve human activity or human judgment.

The SSM is a way to acknowledge the subjectivity or willfulness that is a central characteristic of human behavior and to still treat it in a rigorous manner. The model attempts to model only those business processes that are relevant to the issue or problem being investigated. Checkland calls this the *relevant system.* It is constructed through a process of discovery, debate, and review that happens among the people who actually operate the system. Since any system definition is inherently subjective, this process allows for a model that will be understood and accepted by the greatest number of people.

In the SSM, the central definition or name of a system is always expressed as a transformational activity that turns some set of inputs into a specific set of outputs. For instance, a system could be named "New Product Development System" or "Health Care Delivery System."

Systems are modeled as the collection of subsystems or processes and the relationships among processes that are needed to turn the system's inputs into the system's outputs. The individual processes of the system are mapped out and the relationships between them are drawn in. These relationships show the flows of information, money, people, and material that occur between each process.

Often, these process maps have several levels. A high-level map shows the major processes in the system. Then lower-level maps for each process show more detailed pictures of the subprocesses within the high-level processes.

Once the relevant system showing the existing state of operations is defined, the next step is to create a model showing the ideal state of the relevant system. Again, this ideal model is shaped and refined as it goes through a process of comment and review by the people who will be affected by it. When an ideal model is agreed upon, the work to be done is identified by the differences between the existing relevant model and the ideal relevant model. (See Exhibit 3.3.)

Peter Senge's book, *The Fifth Discipline: The Art and Practice of the Learning Organization,* built on the SSM and, in particular, it explored the potential of systems thinking as a learning paradigm. He advocates the use of systems maps—diagrams that show the key elements of systems and how they connect.

EXHIBIT 3.3   SOFT SYSTEMS MODEL: MULTILEVEL
PROCESS MAPS

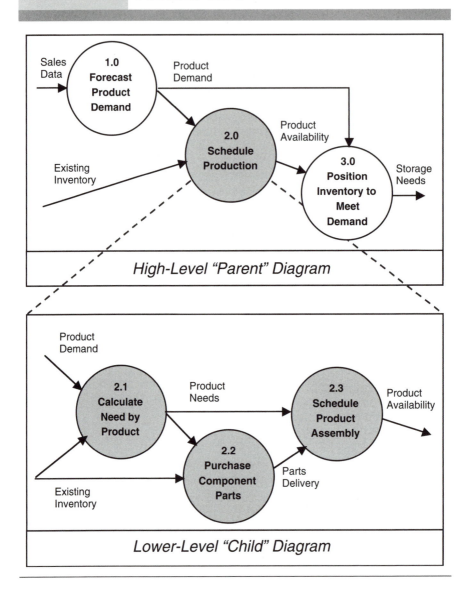

High-Level "Parent" Diagram

Lower-Level "Child" Diagram

People need to learn to see the complex systems in which they work and be able to appreciate the system dynamics that are involved. Failure to understand the system dynamics that shape their situation leads people into the trap of blaming others for their problems and feeling powerless to fix them. Senge says that while all people have the capacity to learn, many people find themselves in organizations where they have no opportunity or encouragement to learn, so they remain trapped in old ways of doing things.

Senge shows how systems thinking is the foundation upon which people and an entire organization learn to change and continuously adapt to their changing environment. He shows how the system dynamics that exist in a system are the product of different combinations of positive- and negative-feedback loops among different system processes.

In order to avoid the judgmental meaning that people place on the words *positive* and *negative,* Senge uses the terms *reinforcing feedback* for positive feedback and *balancing feedback* for negative feedback. Reinforcing feedback refers to the fact that positive feedback creates a snowballing or self-reinforcing effect. Balancing feedback refers to the way that negative feedback causes a process to seek a predefined objective or a state of being that is defined as equilibrium.

DESIGNING THE REAL-TIME ENTERPRISE

The challenge of the coming decades is to find new organizational structures that are better suited for success in a real-time world than the traditional hierarchy. The narrowly focused view of the world and the slow response times characteristic of a hierarchy undermine a company's ability to handle complexity and move quickly. New structures for organizations are needed.[9]

As we start designing and experimenting with real-time organization structures, the VSM and the SSM offer useful insights and techniques. Concepts from systems dynamics and cybernetics provide guidelines to use in formulating operating policies for these organizations.

The VSM is focused largely on optimizing system performance. It defines an optimal organization structure and control process for organizations to employ. The SSM focuses more on the learning process that a company needs to go through. It provides people with a learning process that enables them to discover root causes of problems in their company and design new processes that effectively respond to those problems.

We can benefit from combining the strengths of both approaches. People can use the SSM as a methodology for collecting the information they need to construct a VSM that is relevant to their situation. The SSM also provides a process for widespread input and review from people as the ideal system is designed.

The VSM provides us with the tools and cybernetic principles needed to design an ideal system that will have the requisite variety to deal effectively with its environment. This model helps us as we get into specific designs. It reminds us that the system being designed needs to have certain capabilities if it is going to survive and thrive.

Let's start our investigation of a real-time organization by using the SSM and Senge's system notation to draw out the high-level dynamics that will drive our new organization, as shown in Exhibit 3.4. It is composed of three high-level feedback loops. One of them is a balancing feedback loop and one of them is a reinforcing feedback loop. The third feedback loop oscillates between balancing and reinforcing, depending on whether standard business procedures are being maintained as they are or whether these procedures are being updated with a new procedure that has proven to be effective.[10]

System dynamics created by the interplay among these three feedback loops provide the organization with its ability to be successful. The company receives a wide range of market and customer input and employs a set of standardized business processes to respond to them. Complexity is recognized when data or events occur that are exceptions to the standard business process rules.

Inputs that are not expected or cannot be handled by the standardized processes are flagged, and appropriate people are alerted to examine the data. The reason for data that is an exception to a standard set of rules will be either because of an error in the data or because the data reflect something new that is out of the routine. The people who are alerted will decide whether the nonstandard data is the result of an input or process error or if it indicates something new in the environment. (See Exhibit 3.4.)

If the nonstandard data is the result of an error (loop 1), then people investigate and eliminate root causes of error. If the nonstandard data is the result of something new (loop 2), then people investigate that and respond by creating new business processes. If these new processes lead to business suc-

EXHIBIT 3.4   THE REAL-TIME ENTERPRISE IS A PROCESS, NOT A THING

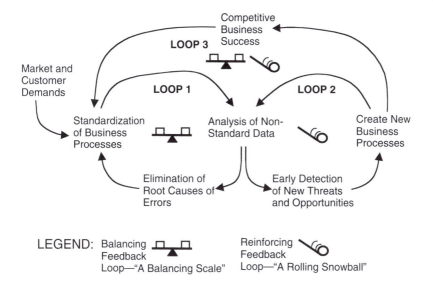

This diagram illustrates the system dynamics that drive a real-time company. The company standardizes and systematizes its business processes to maximize operating efficiencies. Inputs of nonstandard or nonroutine data are identified immediately and brought to the attention of appropriate people.

Nonstandard data is created either by errors in the data or by appearance of something new (threat or opportunity). If the data or the business process shows an error, root-cause analysis fixes errors at the source making the standard business processes even more efficient. If the data shows a new development, then early detection allows time to create new business processes to respond.

Those new business processes that deliver business success become part of the standardized business process of the company. Over time, these new procedures change the structure and behavior of the company itself.

cess, then they become part of the standardized business processes of the company (loop 3).

Through this systems dynamic the organization itself does not have a static structure. It continues to evolve over time as its customers and markets evolve. This characteristic of continuous evolution of the organizational structure is one of the key concepts in designing a real-time enterprise.

THE POTENTIAL OF THE SELF-ADJUSTING BUSINESS UNIT

A self-adjusting business unit depends on a continuous flow of real-time data to monitor its performance. This performance monitoring generates balancing (or negative) feedback that drives the self-adjusting feedback loop. It is illustrated in Exhibit 3.4 as loop 1. This is the most obvious place for organizations to start experimenting with real-time designs. The balancing feedback loop is the most common type of feedback loop, and it is the most important to a company's survival in the short to midterm time frames. Balancing feedback loops allow an organization to continuously maximize the performance of any given operation and to steer itself toward a predefined target or destination.

The viable systems model tells us that we need to create operating units that have maximum autonomy to make decisions and operate within agreed-upon performance ranges. Using balancing feedback loops, people can learn to make existing systems and procedures more and more efficient. Using techniques from operations research, six sigma, and business process management, people can constantly improve the efficiency of operating systems and steer them toward performance levels defined as six sigma (see Exhibit 2.5).

An effective approach to real-time operations is to use relatively simple and standardized processes to handle the vast majority of business transactions and use computer systems to automate the routine transactions. When a nonroutine event happens, these systems do not attempt to handle it. They simply flag those exceptions and alert the appropriate people.

By using simple information systems and standardized work procedures to handle routine operations, companies get good economies of scale as the volume of their business transactions grows. They also avoid the cost and risks associated with building and using more complex information systems. It is the very simplicity of the systems and procedures that makes it easier to constantly improve their performance.

This approach also allows companies to best leverage the skills and talents of their employees. People are very good at analysis and problem solving. We don't need computers to think for us. We like investigating and solving interesting and nonroutine problems. Our brains have been evolving for 200,000 years to do just that. We love to devour information, search for patterns, and make comparisons. Each nonroutine problem that people investigate provides data for ongoing root-cause analysis, resulting in further error reduction and greater efficiencies in business processes.

The industrial revolution was born when we learned to harness the power of the steam engine to the production process. In the steam engine we had a movable and controllable power source that could be harnessed to do the work required to make huge numbers of products much more efficiently than anything ever seen before. Because these products became available at prices that many more people could afford, there was then a great demand for them. A self-reinforcing cycle of prosperity began to take hold.

By the same token, great wealth will again be created when we learn to harness the power of the self-adjusting feedback loop to the processes that drive the operations of a company or a whole economy. As this happens, companies—and eventually entire economies—will start to operate on an entirely new level of efficiency and responsiveness.

By applying the dynamics of self-adjusting feedback loops to business processes, we will produce a steady stream of error corrections and productivity enhancements to those processes. It will be like the effect of compound interest on capital over time. The cumulative result will create much better profits and much less waste. This will generate another self-reinforcing cycle of prosperity.

THOUGHT LEADER INTERVIEW

ORGANIZATIONAL CONTROL AND VALUE CREATION

Sally Helgesen is an internationally recognized writer, speaker, coach, and consultant. She examines how changes in technology, demographics, and economic forces combine to create new definitions of work and how this affects the practice of leadership. She has written a number of best-selling books, including *The Female Advantage: Women's Ways of Leadership* and *The Web of Inclusion: A New Architecture for Building Great Organizations*. The *Wall Street Journal* chose *The Web of Inclusion* as one of the five best books on leadership ever written.

She has consulted extensively for the United Nations, helping them to apply more decentralized models of leadership for programs in Africa and Asia. Sally was a Visiting Scholar at Northwestern University and has taught at the Harvard Graduate School of Education and Smith College. She holds a degree in classics from Hunter College.

"There is an interesting paradox that is occurring in business. On one hand we know that we need to get beyond the centrally controlled hierarchy, yet at the same time there has actually been more centralizing of power and decision making in many large corporations." Sally explained that this is because investors who want only short-term profits drive the stock markets and they punish companies that take a long-term view. "Our markets encourage senior managers to centralize operations, cut costs, cash out, and move on." Managers learn ways to create short-term earnings boosts in companies but these earnings cannot be sustained over the long term.

Few companies at present can resist this dynamic. One example of a company that can resist is Intel. "Intel is an interesting example", said Sally. "They can still think long term when most companies cannot. They can do this because they have achieved such dominance in their marketplace. Andy Grove [their CEO] knew that they had to position themselves as a dominant player in order to generate the revenue stream that would maintain their ability to experiment and build for the future. This revenue stream supports a continual stream of innovation. It let them move from the 8086 chip to the 80286, to the '386, the '486, and then the Pentium line. Otherwise, they would be just another chip maker pressured by the stock market to boost earnings by slashing R&D [research and development] and increasing production efficiencies of existing chip sets. In other words, they would become a commodity."

Because of this stock market dynamic, we are caught at the moment in an economy that is creating large concentrations of wealth in the hands of big investors and senior corporate managers. "We had assumed that becoming a knowledge worker was the path to prosperity, but the market now undervalues the knowledge worker because that work is so easy to outsource and outsourcing is a fast, short-term way to cut costs and boost profits. Ironically, skilled blue-collar workers such as plumbers, carpenters, and electricians are more secure than many white-collar workers. They know that the demand for their talents will continue because in many areas there is a shortage of people with these skills and their work cannot be outsourced to a low-cost country—it must be done locally."

Sally observed that in much of the world, people have figured out that the best type of government is an inclusive democracy, not a centralized dictatorship. And people also know that the kind of economy they want cannot be centrally controlled either. Yet, at present, economic trends are creating more, not less centralized control. "Capitalism is about controlling the means of production, and capitalism spread during the industrial revolution when the work of humans became centralized and commoditized. There is still a strong trend to further commoditize labor by using technology as a means to micromanage people and thus control their production.

"This trend cannot be sustained. It misunderstands the relationship between labor and wealth creation. Attempts to use technology in a Big Brother way is a regressive attempt to maintain control over the means of production." The commoditizing and dumbing down of labor must be accompanied by the increasing complexity of the technology used for control. "At some point the whole thing collapses," Sally pointed out. "Motivated people using simple technology will outdo unmotivated people using complex technology. Complexity makes people feel over-whelmed and unempowered."

Another factor that counterbalances the rise of technical complexity and centralized control is the entry of women into the workforce around the world. "Women in the workplace often take a different approach to work. They are not as impressed by complex technology as men often are. They are more focused on just using technology to get things done. To them, the trend of increasing complexity is much less interesting. Complexity really straitjackets people's interactions, and women are often interested in finding flexible and inclusive ways of working together.

"In my book *The Web of Inclusion* I explored ways that companies get ongoing innovation in their products and processes. Innovation is certainly not centralized at the top. For instance, the "Intel Inside" advertising logo came from a lower-level marketing group in Denver and some trademark lawyers, not from Intel senior management. Another example was Beth Israel Hospital in Boston. It was the nurses that came up with the patented ideas for special bandages and medical equipment. Nurses, not top management, came up with these ideas because they were the ones who dealt with the patients."

Sally believes that, in the end, centralized control and the technical complexity that supports it become self-defeating because they suppress innovation. "Obviously, innovation is the key to a company's survival. In today's economy things are quickly commoditized. Once things are created, they are easy to copy and then they can be manufactured in low-wage countries. It is only the free flow of ideas and personal interactions that happen in a web of inclusion that enables a company to innovate new products and services. Without this innovation, the company's offerings become commodities, and its profits are destroyed by endless price wars."

ENDNOTES

1. Jay Forrester, *Industrial Dynamics* (Cambridge, MA: Pegasus Communications, 1961).
2. Stafford Beer, *The Heart of Enterprise* (New York: John Wiley & Sons, 1979), p. 372.
3. Peter Checkland, *Systems Thinking, Systems Practice: Includes a 30 Year Retrospective* (New York: John Wiley & Sons, 1999).
4. Society for Organizational Learning (2004), *http://www.solonline.org/aboutsol/purposes/*.
5. Peter Senge, *The Fifth Discipline: The Art and Practice of The Learning Organization* (New York: Doubleday/Currency, 1990).
6. A good overview of Forrester's writings is provided by F. Heylighen, "Cybernetics and Systems Thinkers," in F. Heylighen, C. Joslyn, and V. Turchin (eds.), *Principia Cybernetica Web* (Brussels: Principia Cybernetica), *http://pespmc1.vub.ac.be/REFERPCP.html*.
7. Stafford Beer, *Brain of the Firm* (New York: John Wiley & Sons, 1981); and *The Heart of Enterprise* (New York: John Wiley & Sons, 1981).
8. Peter Checkland, *Systems Thinking, Systems Practice* (New York: John Wiley & Sons, 1981).
9. A book that further explores the forces that shape societies, economies, and organizations is written by Mark Buchanan, *Nexus: Small Worlds and the Groundbreaking Science of Network* (New York: W. W. Norton & Company, 2002).
10. A book that offers useful insights for designing business systems to operate in a complex world is written by Jamshid Gharajedaghi, *Systems Thinking: Managing Chaos and Complexity, A Platform for Designing Business Architecture* (Boston, MA: Butterworth Heinemann, 1999).

CHAPTER 4

Embracing Change

We continue to make the mistake of thinking of systems as just technology. Actually, systems are the result of the interplay among people, business processes, and technology. Everything starts with people. If people do not embrace new technology and devise new business processes to best use what the technology can do, then there will be no benefits gained.

What can companies do to ensure that their people support the changes needed to use new technology for competitive advantage? This chapter explores that question and offers some answers. Significant change in organizational structure and behavior is an inescapable part of the transition to the real-time enterprise.

CHANGE IS A GIVEN

In spite of everything that has happened in business and technology since the early 1980s, many of us (myself included) have perhaps secretly wished that we could find a job that was orderly and comfortable and didn't change much. We could learn the ropes and then settle back for an easy ride. Alas, the world has gone in a different direction.

The world we live in now is driven by the convergence of a host of powerful forces. These forces are transforming the way we live, how we do business, and how our societies are organized. We all know what the forces are: globalization, increasing economic competition, outsourcing of white-collar and professional jobs, movement of manufacturing to low-wage countries, global warming . . . the list goes on.

Along with this, though, many things are now possible that could not be done before. The only thing that is truly impossible is to resist change and not evolve with the times. Yet change need not be a relentless and harshly demanding process. We can learn to "do change." It can even be lots of fun from time to time.

We are sailors on the oceans created by this convergence of forces, and our organizations are the ships we sail. We cannot sail against the prevailing winds, but we can set our sails and work with the winds to reach the destinations we want to reach. Just as sailors learn to use the wind and the waves to get where they want to go, so the rest of us can learn to use change to our advantage. It is in this learning that some our greatest opportunities lie.

For Peter Senge, real learning gets to the heart of what it is to be human. We become able to re-create ourselves. This applies to both individuals and organizations. For a learning organization it is not enough to just survive. In Senge's words, "Survival learning or what is more often termed 'adaptive learning' is important—indeed it is necessary. But for a learning organization, 'adaptive learning' must be joined by 'generative learning,' learning that enhances our capacity to create."[1]

Economic success in the real-time world calls for a combination of innovation and the willingness of people to learn new skills. This requires effort on the part of people and the courage not to give up when the going gets tough. We can no longer fall back on the old, familiar, and now outmoded methods of the Industrial Age. Open-minded and observant companies can and will learn. They will survive and thrive. Charles Darwin observed that "It is not the strongest of the species that survive, nor the most intelligent, but the ones most responsive to change."[2]

CHANGE CREATES FEAR— WHY COMPANIES FAIL

In my experience there are two main reasons why attempts at change do not succeed. Both reasons arise from fear. They each create reinforcing feedback loops that cause fear to grow stronger. And as fear grows stronger, the organization's ability to change grows weaker until it finally comes to a halt. I have seen this fear and its manifestations cause people to resist change, even though it is obvious to all that without change the organization will die. I have seen people win the battle against change only to have the world pass them by if not completely run them over.

The first reason for failure is a lack of personal trust within organizations. When change is proposed there is a need to maintain and build the trust of those who will be affected. People wonder what the new way of doing things will mean to their status, to their jobs, and to their incomes. If the information and communication needed to answer those questions is not available or is edited and incomplete, then trust is not possible. In the absence of trust, fear will permeate everything and every move will be resisted.

Military people have known for centuries that soldiers do not fight for abstract ideas such as patriotism and honor. They fight because of the mutual trust and respect that exists among them and the other members of the tactical unit of which they are a part. They do what needs to be done because of bonds of mutual trust and respect. They cannot bear the thought of letting down their buddies, and they know in turn that their buddies will not let them down.

If these bonds of trust are broken, then no one will move. No one will take a risk. The entire unit will be unable to do even the simplest of things. No amount of ordering and threatening by officers will produce much in the way of desirable results.

A basic level of trust among people in a company is indispensable for any chance at effective change. People need to believe that their interests will be looked out for and that there is a place for them in whatever change is happening. If the officers of a company hide information and attempt to fool people into going along with something that will result in their downsizing or outsourcing or simple dismissal, then there will be no enthusiasm and only grudging cooperation from most people. Management can carve up the company and sell off units and assets, but that is just cashing out. It is not true organizational change.

The second reason for failure to make effective changes is management itself. The employees of a company are no more responsible for the failure to change than the common soldier is responsible for the failure to win a battle. In both cases, the responsibility for and the causes of failure clearly reside with those in charge.

We have all seen attempts at organizational change in which management "talks the talk, but doesn't walk the walk." What causes managers to do this? I believe that in most cases this behavior also is motivated by fear. Managers may intellectually believe that change is necessary, but emotionally there is a deep feeling of insecurity and uneasiness that effectively prevents anything more than lip service to change.

Many managers became managers because they were good at skills and behaviors that may not be so valuable after an organization changes. Many managers are not sure that they can reinvent themselves or learn new skills. They are threatened by people who have the skills and behavior needed to be creative and to be successful at leading change. They fear that those people will replace them or somehow render them less powerful.

The tendency to obstruct change can in many cases be most pronounced in the middle ranks of a company. People with titles that range from supervisor to director often have the most to lose in an organizational change. The impact of a proposed change may fall more on them than it does on senior managers. Senior managers can be quite committed to making a change, but it is the middle managers who are in a position to either make it happen on a daily basis, ignore it, or slow it down in a hundred small ways.

If a company expects to make the kind of change that is called for to become a truly effective real-time enterprise, then its managers, from supervisors to CEOs, need to be committed and confident about doing the work that is required. All levels of management must see advantages for themselves and for their careers in the proposed change. If some managers fear a change for whatever reason, those fears must be identified and addressed. If not, the management of a company will be working against itself, and the message that sends to the rest of the organization is, "Management is not really serious about change." (See Exhibit 4.1.)

You "Gotta Wanna"

It is the management of an organization that is responsible for creating successful change. As the saying goes, you "gotta wanna" or else you "ain't gonna." Organizations cannot grudgingly make small changes one at a time and expect to successfully transform themselves. The move from a centrally controlled hierarchy to an effective real-time enterprise of autonomous operating units is a significant transformation for any organization to make.

Change is an evolutionary journey. Once the process starts, if it is to be successful, it will continue on and on. There can be pauses. The pace of change can and must vary, but there can be no stopping. Since change happens anyway (we all get older whether we want to or not), the successful

EXHIBIT 4.1   WHY ORGANIZATIONS FAIL TO CHANGE

LACK OF PERSONAL TRUST	LACK OF MANAGEMENT COMMITMENT
• People need to trust that their interests are being looked out for.	• Managers often "talk the talk" but do not "walk the walk."
• People need to trust that there is a place for them in the new order of things.	• Managers often became managers due to skills that may be devalued by change.
• If there is no trust, then fear will be pervasive.	• Managers may fear a loss of control and prestige.
• Fear causes people to resist change.	• Fear causes managers to undermine change.

company takes the approach of working with change instead of letting a changing world pass it by.

Employees in many companies are quite willing to try something new. I see plenty of frustration and boredom when I walk through the "cube farms" of a typical corporate office. I see people sitting in small cubicles looking into computer screens. I see people doing repetitive tasks that often involve reviewing documents to find small errors and then fixing the same small errors and processing the same documents over and over again. This is not work that is challenging or rewarding. It does not exercise the full range of skills that most people possess. This kind of work is stupefying.

In their life outside of work, people raise children, participate in community organizations, and have skills and interests that they have developed and expanded over many years. They have a lot of talent to bring to bear in their jobs if there is a chance to do so. If people see that their managers are sincere about finding new ways to do things, they will participate in the hope that they can make their jobs more satisfying.

It is also true that the last couple of decades have seen one trendy idea after another sweep through companies. Many of these ideas have been good ones. In Chapter 2, we discussed some of them: total quality management, six sigma, lean manufacturing, and business process reengineering. Yet employees have reason to be cynical. All of these ideas were introduced with great fanfare, grew for a while, and then faded away to be replaced by another idea. Nobody likes to be fooled into participating in something that will only dry up and blow away.

Many organizations are ripe for change. Employees are willing, economic pressure is relentless, new ideas are in the air, and the technology exists to implement these ideas. All that is needed is for those in charge to clearly demonstrate that they are committed to change.

WHAT IS LEADERSHIP?

Few words are more frequently used in business than the words *leadership* and *leader.* Another common pair of words is *managing* and *managers.* In many instances we use the words *leader* and *manager* as if they were interchangeable. This creates a lot of confusion because the two words are not interchangeable.

There is a distinct difference between leading and managing. Let's start with a definition of the two. John Kotter is a professor at the Harvard Business School who has investigated and thought at length about leadership and organizational change. He offers the following definitions for management and leadership (the italics are mine):

- *Management* is a set of processes that can keep a complicated system of people and technology running smoothly. The most important aspects of management include planning, budgeting, organizing, staffing, controlling, and problem solving.

- *Leadership* is a set of processes that creates organizations in the first place or adapts them to significantly changing circumstances. Leadership defines what the future should look like, aligns people with that vision, and inspires them to make it happen despite the obstacles.[3]

Both leaders and managers are needed in an organization if that organization is to be a viable system and succeed over the long run. The relative influence of leaders and managers in an organization will ebb and flow as an organization adapts to its environment. The point here is to recognize that people each have their own skill sets. Do not expect managers to do the work of leaders and do not expect leaders to do managers' work. To do so is a fundamental mistake that renders all further action ineffectual. (See Exhibit 4.2.)

EXHIBIT 4.2   LEADERSHIP AND MANAGEMENT

LEADERSHIP	MANAGEMENT
generates a reinforcing feedback loop that creates new ways of doing things	controls a balancing feedback loop that enhances and fine-tunes existing ways of doing things

Leadership and management are distinctly different processes. Some people are better at leading and some are better at managing. Do not ask managers to do the work of leaders, and do not expect leaders to do the work of managers.

Leaders generate the reinforcing feedback loops that build new things, and managers control the balancing feedback loops that drive the accuracy and productivity of business operations. This means that leaders are needed at first to start a cycle of change and new growth.[4] If the change is successful, it will create whole new ways of doing things as well as whole new things to do. Then managers are needed to consolidate the gains made. Managers will need to enhance and fine-tune the operations of the new business processes that were created.

And then, using the efficient new operations as a base, the organization needs to branch out and continue creating. This is the only way to keep up with a changing world. It is the way living organisms behave. At any given moment, a viable organization is engaged in two things simultaneously: It is reaping the rewards of its existing operations by continuously enhancing and fine-tuning them, and it is exploring its environment and building new operations to capitalize on new opportunities.

CREATING A PROCESS OF CHANGE

When a company wants to start a cycle of change, it needs to activate a process for generating and guiding the reinforcing feedback loop that enables an organization to create something new. In order for that process to be successful, we know that it must be supported by a viable system. The viable systems model (VSM) tells us that this system must be able to create, implement, and regulate its own operations. In business terms, that means that successful change is enabled by groups of people who have the authority to make decisions and who have the resources they need to act and get things done.

The specific way that this change process is implemented in an organization depends on its unique situation and circumstances. Each organization must make its own decisions, but in the end every change process has to do the same things. Leaders, not managers, must be appointed to lead the change process. These people must be given the authority and resources they need to make decisions, take action, and get things done. This is true whether the change process is for a single business unit or for an entire corporation.

EIGHT STAGES IN THE CHANGE PROCESS

Much has been written and said about enabling change. In his book *Leading Change,* John Kotter lays out what he calls the "eight-stage change process." This process has come to be recognized as a standard by many people. The eight stages are: [5]

1. Establishing a sense of urgency
2. Creating the guiding coalition
3. Developing a vision and strategy
4. Communicating the change vision
5. Empowering a broad base of people to take action
6. Generating short-term wins
7. Consolidating gains and producing even more change
8. Institutionalizing new approaches in the culture

In the change process, people may be operating in many of these stages at the same time, but each stage needs to occur to make it possible for the next one to happen. Let's take a quick look at each of them.

Establishing a Sense of Urgency

Establishing a sense of urgency is needed to overcome the inertia or complacency that exists in an organization before a change. If organizational complacency is not removed, it will act to obstruct and prevent change. Systems theory reminds us that complex systems—such as any business organization—are intent on maintaining homeostasis (their internal equilibrium).

In this phase, people need to be informed of the situation facing the company. They need to understand the nature of the threats and the opportunities that confront them and the company. It often takes a crisis to get people's attention or to get them to take their situation seriously. Good leaders find ways to raise the urgency level. They can let a small crisis happen by not fixing something and letting it fail. Or they can induce a crisis by setting goals that the company cannot currently accomplish and forcing people to acknowledge that shortcoming.

Creating the Guiding Coalition

A coalition of people is necessary to guide the change process. It is not possible for one leader to do this all alone. Even if this individual is a powerful CEO, that person needs to recruit the active assistance of a group of people with the skills and operational influence to make change happen. Even worse than a single person's attempting to create change on his or her own is for a bureaucratic committee to try to legislate change. A dedicated individual can at least communicate his or her passion. A committee cannot do even that. People do not take committees seriously in these situations.

To build a guiding coalition, the leader needs to find the right people, create shared trust among these people, and facilitate the development of a common goal that everyone can commit to. Finding the right people means assembling a group of people who have the needed authority, expertise, and credibility to deal with the issues that will arise. Shared trust will develop if communication is frank and comprehensive and it is clear that everyone will benefit from change.

Developing a Vision and Strategy

In John Kotter's words, "Vision refers to a picture of the future with some implicit or explicit commentary on why people should strive to create that future."[6] Vision is important because it is a way to coordinate and motivate the actions of large numbers of people. Because a good vision enables everyone to see where the company is going and why, groups of people are able to act autonomously and still coordinate their actions and move toward common goals. The viable systems model discussed in Chapter 3 calls for operating units in a business to operate as autonomously as possible. This is possible only if an organization has a clear vision.

Without a clear vision that everyone understands, senior management of a company must issue authoritarian edicts to get people moving, and then they must send a constant stream of detailed instructions for what everyone should do at every step along the way. This may work to some degree for maintaining existing operations and policies, but it cannot work to guide a company through a major change. There is too much to do for one person or one small group of people to figure it all out. Everyone must buy in and do the necessary thinking in their own areas of responsibility. It is also important for people to understand the long-term benefits of doing something that, in the short term, will probably make their lives more difficult. In Chapter 3, we saw how, when changes are made to complex systems, long-term benefits entail working through short-term problems.

Communicating the Change Vision

Given the amount of information that flows through our lives, we tend to assign importance to an issue depending on the amount of information and the frequency of communications we receive regarding an issue. If people are to take something seriously, they need to hear a lot about it and they need to hear about it often. Otherwise, issues that may truly be important do not stand out from the constant clutter of information that fills our lives.

Effective communication calls for messages to be in simple language that everyone can understand. Messages must be free of technical terms and jargon that has meaning only to a smaller group of people. Colorful metaphors can be particularly effective in communicating an idea in a few well-chosen words. The change vision needs to be communicated frequently in large and small meetings, and it should be communicated using different media, from newsletters to videos.

Perhaps the most important and effective means of communication is simply the behavior of those in charge. People will watch closely to see if senior management acts in such a way that shows they really believe in and support the change vision. If they are deemed to be insincere about the vision, then the rest of the organization will also be insincere.

Empowering a Broad Base of People to Take Action

Once people understand the change vision, how do you get them to act? Kotter says that the change leader needs to look at four things and make sure those four things are properly aligned to support the actions people need to take. Those four things are structures, skills, systems, and supervisors.

Structures refer to the organizational departments and business units. Skills refer to the personal capabilities of the people in the organization and those capabilities they will need to be successful at change. Systems refer to the processes—from purchasing to product development, from training to employee evaluation—that are used to get things done. Supervisors are the people who manage business units within the organization.

For change to be effective it usually means that the structure of the organization will change. The change leader must ensure that people have the authority and resources they need to change company structures or those structures will prevent change. Change usually means that people will need to learn new skills. They must get the training they need, or else they will not be able to act effectively. Operating policies and the systems that support them will also have to change. Again, people must be given the authority and resources to make these changes, or else the old ways of doing things will continue to reassert themselves.

Supervisors or middle managers are the people who will either enable and guide the change activities, or they will oppose and undermine change. The middle managers in a company are often the ones most impacted by change and the ones who often fear they have the most to lose. As noted earlier in the chapter, if those leading change do not effectively address the fears and concerns of middle managers, then there will be no change.

Generating Short-Term Wins

Grand visions, effective communication, and empowered people taking action make for a good start. But all this activity must create clear benefits and demonstrable value in the near term—about two years or less. It is these short-term wins that validate the change vision. Since there are always people who doubt that change can succeed, these wins are needed to build support. Short-term wins give the change leader the credibility and momentum needed to keep the change process moving ahead.

In addition to validating the change leader's vision, Kotter points out that these short-term wins provide a number of other benefits. They offer an opportunity to reward the people who achieved these successes, and they build the morale of everyone involved. They also provide valuable experience that can be used to fine-tune the vision and strategies. People can incorporate what they learned from one success into their plan to achieve the next success. Finally, these wins provide the bosses or backers of the change leader with the evidence they need to see that the change effort is on track. It shows them that they are backing a winner.

Consolidating Gains and Producing Even More Change

Generating short-term wins is key to building the momentum that drives organizational change. It is also important to watch out for the tendency to let short-term wins reduce people's sense of urgency. Those leading change need to use these gains to create even more change. Otherwise, the early gains made in an organizational change effort get confused with reaching the longer-term goals. If those leading change do not keep up the sense of urgency, momentum is lost.

Change leaders must continue to focus on helping everyone understand the vision and the strategies the company is using to accomplish its goals. To keep up momentum, change leaders and their guiding coalitions build on the credibility gained from short-term wins. They use each win as a base from which to launch even more changes, and they bring even more people into the various change initiatives that are under way.

The way that momentum continues to build is for more and more change projects to be launched. The only way that many simultaneous projects can be done successfully is for the guiding coalition to delegate the project management and related decisions to those actually doing the work. The change leader supports these projects by eliminating unneeded interdependencies between projects. This way, they have freedom to act on their own without getting tangled up in constraints over which they have no control. This is the autonomy of operating units that the VSM calls for.

Institutionalizing New Approaches in the Culture

Leaders and change coalitions have to mold the culture of their organizations so that the changes they make are accepted and adopted throughout the organization. This step comes last because it depends on the results and credibility that are delivered by success. Getting everyone in an organization to fully adopt new approaches is possible only after the success of these new approaches has been repeatedly demonstrated and it is clear to all that they are superior to the old ways of doing things.

Culture change involves a lot of discussion, and leaders need to point out why the new approaches worked and give the support and approval that people need in order to give up previously held concepts and adopt new ones. Care must be taken to recruit and promote people who fully embrace the new ways of doing things.

THOUGHT LEADER INTERVIEW

LEADERSHIP AND ORGANIZATIONAL CHANGE

Peter Senge is a senior lecturer at the Massachusetts Institute of Technology, Sloan School of Management, and the founding chair of the Society for Organizational Learning (SoL). In 1990 he published a book titled *The Fifth Discipline.* In 1997, *Harvard Business Review* identified it as one of the seminal management books of the past 75 years. He is also a coauthor of four books since then, *The Fifth Discipline Fieldbook, The Dance of Change, Schools That Learn,* and *Presence: Human Purpose and the Field of the Future,* published in March 2004.

Organizational change and the leadership and learning that enable change are subjects that Peter Senge has thought about deeply. He begins by making the point that creating change is as much about the collaboration of people at the middle levels of a company as it is about what we have traditionally called leadership. "It's kind of an irritation, if I can be blunt," he said, "the word *leader* is equated with boss. It carries a very strong message—you're not a leader if you aren't a CEO. Yet many change initiatives don't get started at the top, they start at the middle levels. We've tried to distinguish between executives and leaders.

"What really are the roles of executives and what are the roles of the change leaders in middle management as well as internal networkers who may operate from almost any formal organizational position? In any organization there are initiators of change and there are sustainers of change. We are trying to get at what I call inclusive leadership, which results from the combination of executives and change leaders at all levels.

"You look at nature and you see change everywhere—it is a characteristic of living systems. Nature is always growing something new in the midst of what already exists." Peter explained that there are two types of processes at work in nature or in any complex system. There are what he calls self-reinforcing feedback loops and balancing feedback loops. "Reinforcing feedback loops always lie at the heart of anything new that grows. Yet no more than 5 to 10% of the feedback loops in a company are reinforcing. The rest are balancing processes. A lot of pejorative labels get put on the "resistance to change," but from another perspective it's simply the natural ways that any organization functions to preserve its way of doing things. If these balancing processes did not exist, no work could ever get done."

Change leaders encounter certain challenges again and again. Peter and a group of collaborators explored these challenges in their book *The Dance of Change*. They brought together people from different organizational levels and different business functions such as sales, manufacturing, and finance to discuss their experiences. It began to be clear that many of the challenges to sustaining change recur in diverse settings and revolve around issues like power, measurement systems focused on short-term tangible performance indicators, and the polarization created by overzealous change advocates.

In order for effective change to occur, executives have to accept that the way they exercise power will change. They need to be comfortable with decentralized control. "The simple fact of the matter is that senior management doesn't have its hands on the reigns of control anyway. There is no alternative to distributing power and authority. For example, you need lots of people actively involved with implementing a strategy if it is to succeed. Management cannot implement a new strategy all by itself.

"Executives that I admire are people that spend a lot of time talking up and down the hierarchy, appreciating the ecology of goals and desires of their people. One of the biggest flaws in senior executives is people who don't have a good understanding of front-line operations—people who think they can manage by the numbers." Peter observes that these numbers are measurements that were created for a simpler industrial economy, and they often do not accurately reflect the real value of an organization anymore.

"We are seeing traditional management systems now reaching the point where they no longer deliver much value." He points to Toyota Motors as an example of a company that has taken a new approach to creating value. They have dealt very effectively with the issues of power and measurement, and this enables the organization to continue to change as its markets change. Toyota has no centralized systems of cost management that would allow an executive to set and enforce arbitrary targets for cost control. "They use a networked approach to cost control—this is Deming 101—the people who most need effective cost measures are those closest to the actual processes that are generating the costs. If you create an environment of respect that encourages people's intrinsic desires to do a better job, they will use cost measures more effectively than distant managers with little deep knowledge of the actual processes." Peter sums this up by saying, "If you want to improve your costs, if you want to increase your company's value, you need to improve your company's learning processes at all levels, and create environments of trust where many people can lead in this improvement."

ENDNOTES

1. Peter Senge, *The Fifth Discipline: The Art and Practice of The Learning Organization* (New York: Doubleday/Currency, 1990), p.14.
2. James Drogan, "Automate the Rote, Give People the Creative Stuff to Do," in James Drogan, ed., *Droganbloggin* (2003), *http://www.jmsdrgn.com/2003_10_01_archive.html*.
3. John Kotter, *Leading Change* (Cambridge, MA: Harvard Business School Press, 1996), p. 25.
4. Another very insightful book on the subject of leadership is written by John Heider, *The Tao of Leadership: Lao Tzu's Tao Te Ching Adapted for a New Age* (Atlanta, GA: Humanics Limited, 1985).
5. John Kotter, *Leading Change* (Cambridge, MA: Harvard Business School Press, 1996), p. 33.
6. Ibid., p. 68.

CHAPTER 5

Observe–Orient–Decide–Act

E very real-time organization needs a clearly understood process that it can use to guide its day-to-day operations. This chapter introduces just such a process. It originated in the military as a way to plan and execute attacks. Then numerous people noticed that the same process also applies to the way a company competes in its markets.

This process has great potential to provide companies with the coordination they need to effectively harness the speed provided by self-adjusting, real-time systems. In this chapter we will look at that process and show how companies that aspire to become real-time organizations can use it.

THAT'S HOW THE FIGHTER PILOTS DO IT

Perhaps the epitome of a real-time environment is flying a jet fighter in combat. John Boyd was a jet fighter pilot. He fought in the Korean War, and after the war he became an instructor at the U.S. Air Force's Fighter Weapons School. This school instructs the best pilots in advanced air-to-air combat tactics.

While at the Fighter Weapons School, Boyd had a standing bet with all other fighter pilots. His bet was that regardless of initial starting positions, he would wind up on the other pilot's tail in a weapons-locked-on position within 40 seconds of the start of a dogfight. In these mock dogfights, Boyd would throw his fighter aircraft into one maneuver after another. He performed sequences of moves that his opponents could neither anticipate nor effectively counter. He confused and bewildered the opposing pilots. Word has it that he never lost that standing bet.

Boyd later did research into the results of aerial combat during the Korean War. He noticed that it was not the biggest or fastest aircraft that won dogfights. Instead, it was the most maneuverable aircraft flown by pilots who knew how to use rapid sequences of maneuvers to confuse and defeat their opponents. This research squared with his own experience and he began a life-long quest of research and teaching. His teaching was often viewed as controversial. Much of it has now come to be accepted doctrine in air forces and military organizations around the world. John Boyd's life and ideas are well presented in a book titled *Boyd, The Fighter Pilot Who Changed the Art of War*.[1]

While teaching at the Fighter Weapons School, Boyd authored a paper titled "Aerial Attack Study." In this paper he summarized what he had learned about effective tactics for air-to-air combat. Conventional belief had it that aerial combat was too fast-paced and complex for anyone to ever clearly understand it—it was just instinct, intuition, and luck. Instead, Boyd said that there actually was a set of underlying techniques and that mastering these techniques went a long way toward making a pilot into an ace.

He said that pilots must form a three-dimensional picture of the battle in their heads. Boyd called this "situation awareness." It meant that pilots must know where each of their own squadron's planes is located and where each of the enemy planes is located. Situation awareness requires that a pilot know the position and the velocity of the other planes. The velocity, or the "energy state" as Boyd put it, of an opposing aircraft dictates what maneuvers that aircraft can perform. If a pilot knows the energy state of an opponent, then the pilot also knows the possible moves that the opponent can make and can think of ways to counter each of those moves.

John Boyd left the Fighter Weapons School to attend the Georgia Institute of Technology where he got a degree in industrial engineering. During his studies there, he came upon ideas that led him to formulate an equation to express what he called the "energy-maneuverability" or EM theory. Aeronautical engineers everywhere now use this equation when designing aircraft and evaluating their maneuverability.

The EM theory states that the potential maneuverability of an aircraft at any given moment is determined by its specific energy rate. This is defined as:

$$\text{Specific Energy Rate} = ((\text{Thrust} - \text{Drag}) \,/\, \text{Weight}) \times \text{Velocity}$$

The specific energy rate is calculated by subtracting the aircraft's drag from the thrust generated by its engines, dividing this by the weight of the aircraft, and then multiplying the result by the velocity of the aircraft.[2] This same theory also has potential for describing how a real-time enterprise can maneuver in its business environment (see the Executive Insight section at the end of this chapter).

John Boyd led a lifelong quest to understand and teach others the theory and techniques of what is now called *maneuver warfare*. His teachings are embodied in a learnable and repeatable process that shows individuals and whole organizations how to compete and win in any fast-paced situation. Boyd named this process *observe–orient–decide–act* (OODA). It has come to be known as the *OODA Loop* or the *Boyd Cycle*.

John Boyd died in 1997 and never wrote down his complete set of ideas about the OODA Loop. Over a period of some 20 years, he delivered them in oral presentations. His first presentation was titled "Patterns of Conflict" and lasted about an hour. As he and others who worked with him continued to explore and further articulate these ideas, the presentations grew into a two-day session titled "A Discourse on Winning and Losing."[3]

Real-time information technology is to business organizations as the jet engine is to airplanes. We are now capable of great speed in business. The question is how best to use this capability. The OODA Loop shows us that speed and size alone do not create significant competitive advantage. Maneuverability is what really counts.

MAIN CONCEPTS OF THE OODA LOOP

There are four steps in the OODA Loop. The first step is to observe. This is the process of collecting and communicating information about the environment. The next step is to orient. This is the most important activity because it is where information is turned into an understanding of the situation upon which the next two steps will depend. In this step, the environment is described, the positions of the different players in the environment are defined, and the relevant trends, threats, and opportunities are identified. In the decide step, different responses and plans for implementing them are created and evaluated. The most appropriate response is chosen and that leads to the final step—act. In the act step, action is taken and results occur that are either favorable, not favorable, or indeterminate. These results are picked up in the observe step and the loop continues.

It is important to note that the OODA Loop does not require people or organizations to cycle through all four steps all of the time. It is not a lock-step sequence. Sometimes, when an environment is well understood, the orient and decide steps are not needed. One can simply cycle quickly between observe and act in a series of rapid responses. At other times, one may decide not to act at all and to just observe and orient, waiting for an appropriate opportunity to act. It is better to think of the OODA Loop as an interactive network of activities with the orient step at its core instead of a fixed series of steps. This is illustrated in Exhibit 5.1.

Let's take a closer look at the orient step, since it is the most important. It is the step where a picture of the world is formed, and this picture of the world is what drives the decisions and actions that follow. Good orientation is central to one's ability to take effective action and achieve desirable results.

Each individual or organization will do the orientation step somewhat differently. This step depends on the complex interactions of elements such as one's cultural traditions and heritage, new information, previous experiences, and the analysis and synthesis of all these elements. The process used for orientation is always in a state of change, since it is constantly being affected by feedback from the act step and by new information from the observe step. Differences in the way different people or companies perform

EXHIBIT 5.1   THE OODA LOOP

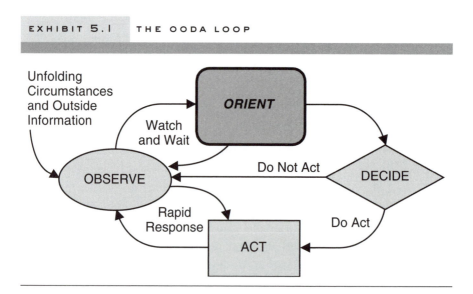

the orient step account for the differences in their reactions to the same environment.

Under pressure, the way an organization performs the orient step can make an enormous difference in its effectiveness. The interaction of the different elements in this step is driven by a positive or reinforcing feedback loop. This results in either an increasing rate of effective and creative responses to a changing environment or to a collapsing sequence of ineffectual and inappropriate actions. Boyd taught that effective competitors in any environment constantly look for mismatches between their initial understanding of the environment and new circumstances as they unfold. In those mismatches there are often opportunities for a competitor to seize new advantages.

The real world unfolds in "an irregular, disorderly, unpredictable manner," as Boyd put it. Those who are able to consistently and effectively use the OODA Loop gain advantages over time. Those who can cycle through the process faster than their competition start to realize an ever-increasing advantage with each cycle. Slower competitors fall farther and farther behind and become less and less able to cope with their deteriorating situations. With each OODA cycle, the actions of the slower competitors become increasingly less relevant or appropriate to the actual circumstances.

Those players who learn to shorten the time needed to observe, orient, decide, and act are the ones who can set the pace and tempo of events. They seize the initiative, and all the other players wind up reacting to their moves. It is not the absolute speed of the cycle that matters but the speed relative to one's competitors. The point is to become faster than your competitors. Differences in speed do not have to be great. Small advantages in speed exploited repeatedly will soon deliver decisive results. At the same time, it is just as important to learn when not to act. Fast execution of ineffective or misguided actions accomplishes nothing.

A major influence on the ideas of the OODA Loop is the ancient Chinese book called *The Art of War*. This book was written some time between 500 and 400 B.C.E. and is attributed to a Taoist philosopher and military theoretician named Sun Tzu. Boyd borrowed heavily from Sun Tzu and incorporated his teachings on the use of orthodox and unorthodox responses—*cheng* and *ch'i*—to master a situation. It is a mixture of the traditional and the unexpected that produces the best results. Traditional, orthodox responses can be implemented very rapidly to counter or exploit certain events. Unexpected, unorthodox responses serve to disorient a competitor and cause the competitor to pause, to question, and to wonder what will happen next. This slows down and stretches out the competitor's OODA Loop cycle time.

Both *The Art of War* and the OODA Loop emphasize the use of ambiguity and deception to disorient the competition. Engaging in activity that is so quick and disorienting that it appears uncertain and ambiguous is a powerful way to shape a situation and influence the actions of a competitor. OODA Loop concepts stress that the target is always the opponent's mind. When the mind of the opponent becomes overwhelmed and dislocated, the battle is won. Sun Tzu states, "Therefore a victorious army first wins and then seeks battle; a defeated army first battles and then seeks victory."[4]

Another major concept of the OODA Loop is that everyone in an effective organization has a common understanding of the organization's purpose and its major objectives. In military organizations this is known as the "commander's intent" or the "mission orders." In other words, people are told what needs to be done but they are not told how to do it. They are not micromanaged; instead, there is trust that they will do the right thing. Within broad predefined parameters, they are free to determine for themselves how they will act. This parallels what the viable systems model (VSM) says about the need for individual operating units in an organization to be as autonomous as possible. It also echoes what was said in Chapter 4 about the need for trust throughout an organization in order for effective change to happen.

The OODA Loop is the sequence that any real-time enterprise uses to respond effectively to its environment. It is a continuous process of moving through the four steps or shortened combinations of these steps as different situations arise. Just as it is the responsibility of jet fighter pilots and military commanders to watch their environments and make decisions about changes in course and operations, it is the responsibility of business executives to watch their markets and do the same. Whether it is a factory, a service group, a division, or a whole company, people leading these business units need to become skilled in using the OODA Loop to guide their organizations in real time.

The OODA Loop is not inherently a balancing process or a reinforcing process. Depending on the orientation and the intent of the people using the process, it oscillates back and forth between a balancing process that takes action to maintain the status quo and a reinforcing process that exploits new opportunities and creates change.

THE AGILE REAL-TIME CORPORATION

As we have seen, maneuverability is more important than either speed or optimizing the performance of any one particular operation. Maneuverability comes from an individual's or an organization's being able to move quickly through the OODA Loop or through subsets of the loop. In business, this ability has come to be called *agility*. Agility enables a company to thrive in a complex and high-change environment.

An agile company is a formidable competitor because it moves so quickly through the OODA Loop. This enables the company to confuse and out-maneuver opposing companies. It takes the initiative and builds market share by sizing up a situation and acting quickly. Then it follows up its first action with more action before its competitors have even finished responding to the first action. In this way, with the completion of every OODA Loop action cycle, the agile company pulls ahead and stays ahead of its competition.

War and business have undeniable similarities, yet it is important to remember that business is not war. War is a process of destruction and it leaves us weakened. War happens because of our failure to find a more constructive response to situations. Business, however, happens because we do find constructive responses to situations. Business is a process of creation and it makes us stronger. Nobody dies. Those who lose have a chance to learn from their experience and try again.

Analogies between war and business are only analogies. If we choose our analogies well and if the analogies are insightful, we can learn from them and then go beyond them. So, with that understanding, let's look at a few useful military analogies.[5]

The ancient Chinese book *The Art of War* by Sun Tzu is a sourcebook that has deeply influenced thinking about maneuverability in warfare and agility in business. Those who wish to develop agility in their own actions and in those of their company are well served by reading *The Art of War* and then reading it again. Agility does not arise from a particular technology or from a specific set of operating techniques. Agility arises from a state of mind, from a way of looking at and responding to the world.

Agility arises from one's ability to respond quickly and creatively to a continuously changing environment. An agile organization focuses on teaching everyone in the organization a clear understanding of an appropriate set of basic concepts. These concepts make it possible for people to quickly orient themselves, make decisions, and take effective action in their respective areas of the business.

Sun Tzu says that the use of simple concepts creatively combined produces a limitless range of possible actions in any situation. This is the essence of agility.

> There are only two kinds of charge in battle, the unorthodox surprise attack and the orthodox direct attack, but variations of the unorthodox and the orthodox are endless. The unorthodox and the orthodox give rise to each other, like a beginningless circle—who could exhaust them?[6]

Agile real-time organizations do not use hierarchical command and control structures. The theory behind the VSM tells us this, and we also see it very clearly in the practices of modern, mobile military organizations such as the U.S. Marine Corps. The basic strategic doctrine of the Marine Corps is put forth in a short, 110-page book titled *Warfighting*.[7] Under the heading "Philosophy of Command," the Marine Corps has this to say (italics are theirs):

> First and foremost, *in order to generate the tempo of operations we desire and to best cope with the uncertainty, disorder, and fluidity of combat, command must be decentralized.* That is, subordinate commanders must make decisions on their own initiative, based on their understanding of their senior's intent, rather than passing information up the chain of command and waiting for the decision to be passed down.[8]

Agile organizations use simple and robust technology, which enables them to deploy new business processes quickly and get effective results. Marine doctrine in *Warfighting* states, "Equipment should be easy to operate and maintain, reliable, and interoperable with other equipment. It should require minimal specialized operator training."[9] It goes on to state, "In order to minimize research and development costs and fielding time, the Marine Corps will exploit existing capabilities—'Off-the-shelf' technology—to the greatest extent possible."[10]

The agile corporation is based on a company culture that incorporates the concepts of the OODA Loop and *The Art of War* and combines them with other concepts that are appropriate to the markets the company serves. Company executives who both talk the talk and walk the walk need to constantly reinforce this culture. Customer service representatives and administrative support people must understand the culture as clearly as group managers and senior executives.

I will offer one more insight into the agile corporation that comes from the conduct of war. The American General George Patton, who certainly understood the power of maneuverability in warfare, said, "Success in war depends on the golden rules of war: speed, simplicity, and boldness."[11]

REINFORCING FEEDBACK FOR CREATING SOMETHING NEW

As the agile corporation moves through its OODA Loop, it is constantly called on to act. At the highest level, action can be thought of as activities that fall into one of two categories. The first category is activity to improve existing operations. The second category is activity to create something new.

Activity in the first category—improve existing operations—is guided by the tactics and techniques embodied in the six sigma DMAIC process (define, measure, analyze, improve, and control; see Chapter 2, Six Sigma section). DMAIC generates a balancing feedback loop. It seeks to move an existing process ever closer to a state of operating efficiency known as six sigma.

Activity in the second category—create something new—is guided by a process that generates a reinforcing feedback loop. The reinforcing feedback loop delivers the focus and momentum needed to develop new things. This activity is guided by a simple three-step process that I call *define–design–build* (DDB).

In the first step—define—people identify a goal and the objectives or the performance requirements that need to be achieved to reach that goal. In this step they also create a conceptual design of the business process or the system that will attain the specified performance requirements or objectives.

Based on this conceptual design, people move into the next step—design. In this step the conceptual design is expanded out to the level of detail necessary to accurately evaluate and implement the proposed new system or business process. Selected technology and procedures are tested for their suitability. Specifications and plans are then created to guide the work of implementation.

In the third step—build—people focus on executing the implementation tasks as rapidly as possible to deliver the required systems and roll out the new business procedures called for in the design step. As the new systems and procedures go into use, objectives are achieved and new situations unfold. People continue working toward their goal by cycling through sequences of these three steps as appropriate. This define–design–build process is illustrated in Exhibit 5.2.

This process is a sequence of steps that increases the momentum of the project at each step. The change, or delta, in the momentum and focus of the project can be objectively measured as work moves from one step to the next. When done successfully, this sequence of steps produces an increase in forward momentum that is as clear as walk–trot–run.

PUTTING IT ALL TOGETHER—DYNAMICS OF THE REAL-TIME ORGANIZATION

A model can be created for the system dynamics of a real-time organization that incorporates the OODA Loop, the six sigma DMAIC process, and the define–design–build sequence. This model of the real-time enterprise combines features of the VSM (see Exhibit 3.2) with the soft systems diagram for a real-time company (see Exhibit 3.4). The VSM (and also the U.S. Marine Corps strategic doctrine) says that a viable organization is com-

---

EXHIBIT 5.2   THREE-STEP DEVELOPMENT PROCESS

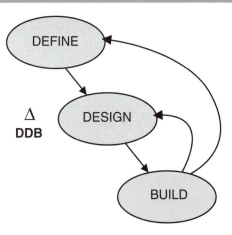

People creating something new go through these three steps. The first step defines the business goal and objectives and creates a conceptual design for a solution. The second step creates a detailed design and implementation plan. The third step builds the solution. Momentum (the delta) increases steadily from one step to the next.

posed of a metasystem for planning and control and a collection of largely autonomous operating units for getting things done.

The Metasystem

The activities of the metasystem are well defined by the four steps in the OODA Loop. The real-time company uses the OODA Loop to navigate through its markets. It is always looking for the mismatches between unfolding circumstances and its own expectations.

The operating units of the real-time organization use standardized and highly automated systems to handle their routine operations. These systems do not attempt to handle anything out of the norm, they simply focus on efficient processing of the day-in, day-out transactions that drive the business. When anything occurs that does not fit into one of the company's standardized operating systems, then it is picked up and reported to the metasystem as an exception.

Management By Exception

The concept of management by exception is nothing new in business, but in the context of the real-time enterprise it is absolutely central to the way the organization works. The real-time enterprise lives in a world of continuous and enormous flow of data. How does it process this data and not become overwhelmed by it? It does this by using a set of standardized business procedures (in effect an autonomic nervous system) that handles all routine transactions automatically with little or no human intervention. The real-time organization devotes its people (its conscious nervous system) to handling only the exceptions.

Exceptions to the norm are another way of describing what Shannon at Bell Labs defined as information. In Chapter 2 we discussed how he defined information as "symbols that contain unpredictable news." As the volume and frequency of data flows increase, humans must focus on the data that contains information and let computers handle the rest.

In the real-time enterprise, automated business process management systems notify appropriate people immediately when exceptions occur. Data inputs that are flagged as exceptions have one of two possible causes. The first possible cause is that the data is incomplete or contains errors. The second possible cause is that the data reflects something new that is out of the routine. This second cause is the kind of mismatch that Boyd talked about, and it needs the company's immediate attention.

People analyze exceptions, not computers. If there are errors in the data, people track down root causes and fix them. If the data is not in error but instead indicates the appearance of something new, then it is very important to have people in the exception-handling loop. This puts them in immediate and intimate contact with the kind of data that indicates a change in market conditions or an emerging threat or opportunity. They can make decisions and act quickly.

When people in the metasystem of an organization make decisions, it means that operating units will be asked to either improve an existing operation (initiate a balancing feedback loop) or create something brand new (initiate a reinforcing feedback loop). The OODA loop itself is an endlessly self-adjusting mix of balancing and reinforcing feedback loops.

Improve an Existing Operation

For actions aimed at improvements in existing operations, the best way to achieve increased efficiencies is to continuously standardize, streamline, and automate routine operations. The six sigma DMAIC process provides guidelines to follow. Business process-mapping methods such as IDEF0 (Integrated Definition Level 0) or BPMN (Business Process Modeling Notation) are tools to enable companies to map out and standardize their routine processes. They enable companies to continuously and iteratively review and streamline processes by eliminating processing steps and sources of error. Business process management systems provide the steady stream of real-time or near real-time data needed to generate balancing feedback loops to fine-tune business processes and constantly nudge them toward six sigma levels of performance.

Create Something New

When a company decides to create something new, the best way to do this is by using the three-step define—design—build process. This is a method for building the momentum required to successfully develop new systems and procedures that will support new operations. Define—design—build is very much a reinforcing feedback loop—a rolling snowball that picks up more speed and more size as it goes. Exhibit 5.3 illustrates the system dynamics of the agile real-time organization.

EXHIBIT 5.3   SYSTEM DYNAMICS OF THE AGILE REAL-TIME ORGANIZATION

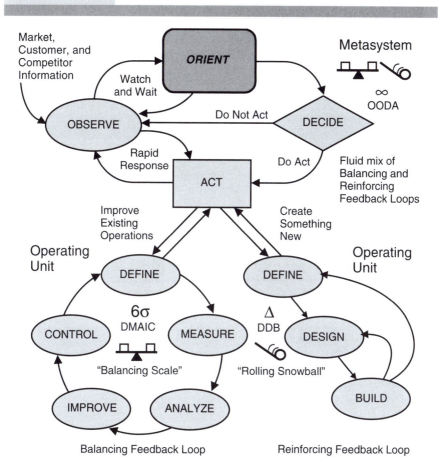

The agile organization continuously observes its environment and orients itself in that environment. Based on orientation, it decides and acts. When it acts, it chooses to either improve existing operations, create something new, or do some mix of the two.

People focused on improving an existing operation engage in a balancing or a fine-tuning process to move the operation toward six sigma performance levels. People focused on creating something new engage in a reinforcing process to generate the momentum needed to create change and develop new systems and procedures.

Building the real-time enterprise calls for a lot of new systems and new procedures to be created. The next four chapters are devoted to this topic. We will look at information technology now available for building real-time systems and also at the leadership required to successfully guide those projects. We will also do a further exploration of the define–design–build process.

EXECUTIVE INSIGHT

VISUAL ORIENTATION IN A REAL-TIME WORLD—"THE FLYBY EFFECT"

New approaches to interacting with the flow of real-time data are called for if we are to make any sense of it all. Merely displaying this data as columns of numbers printed on paper or on computer screens is futile. We have a hard enough time making sense of monthly, quarterly, or yearly summaries of data that are shown as columns of numbers in financial reports. These numbers do not speak clearly to most people, they don't pick up subtle trends very well, and it takes a lot of mental effort to compare the set of numbers for one company with those of another company. What do we do as we move beyond these simple periodic summaries into the continuous flow of data in the real-time world?

In his book, *Brain of the Firm,* Stafford Beer talked about what he called "environments of decision." These environments are used to support the metasystem in his viable systems model. The metasystem performs the functions of looking out at the environment, collecting information, and making predictions and forecasts. It also picks strategies and makes plans to adapt to change. This corresponds to the observe, orient, and decide steps in the OODA Loop.

In describing these environments of decision he said, "In short, everything we know in psychology about perception, pattern recognition, and (in general) awareness of the state of affairs, says that we should try to reach our judgements in terms of relative size and shape, relative color, relative movement." As he described how computers support these environments, he said, "Our control center would leave the handling of digits where this kind of work belongs: inside the computer. Managers would be trained to deal with other kinds of display, essentially graphic, but depending profoundly on relative movement . . ."[12]

Vivek Ranadive is the CEO of a company that makes and sells software products for use by companies needing real-time data distribution to connect internal processes and communicate with trading partners. In 1999 he wrote a book titled *The Power of Now: How Winning Companies Sense & Respond to Change Using Real-Time Technology*. In this book he says, "Grafting exciting user interfaces onto the flow of active information, event-driven systems will present sales reports, for example, as fly-through, 3D landscapes that reflect real-time sales activity".[13]

These people and others have stimulated my thinking about how people can best deal with the massive flows of data that come with living in a real-time world. It is obvious that we need to do something more than print this data out on paper. Whether it is printed as numbers or as charts and graphs, the mere act of printing it will make it obsolete. Time will pass it by. And once the data is printed, it becomes fixed, etched in stone, so to speak. There is no way to interact with it.

What we need to do is to render the data as moving, three-dimensional images and we need to add sound to the moving images as well. We need to fully engage our senses of sight and hearing if we are going to have any hope of effectively coping with the amount of data inherent in the real-time world.

When I read John Boyd's equation for his energy-maneuverability theory, it triggered some additional thoughts. This led to a concept I'll call "The flyby effect." The flyby effect can be used in the orient step of the OODA Loop. It uses an environment of decision composed of moving 3D graphics to display real-time information. I'll illustrate the effect using the example that is shown in Exhibit 5.4.

We begin by noting that a market (or any other space) can be described by a set of three descriptive variables: X, Y, and Z. For this example, let X = gross profit, Y = cost of sales, and Z = revenue. Companies in that market space can then be further described by three more variables: x', y', and z'. In this example, x' = total liabilities, y' = net tangible assets, and z' = total assets.

Each company's X, Y, and Z values (its center point) define its market position. The company itself is shown as an octahedron (an 8-sided 3D object). The size and shape of the octahedron is defined by the values of the company's x', y', and z' variables. If a time series display is made using data collected over time, the position and shape of the companies being displayed will change. This time series display will show company movements within the market space and in comparison to each other. Trends and relationships between the companies will be easy to see. This is illustrated by Exhibit 5.4.

In addition, the flyby effect allows plotting of company trajectories that are accurate predictors of near-term and midterm future positions

EXHIBIT 5.4   THE "FLYBY EFFECT"—VISUAL ORIENTATION
IN A REAL-TIME ENVIRONMENT

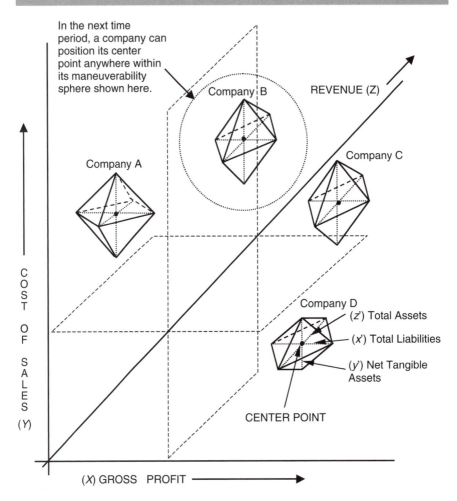

The companies in this market space are represented as octahedrons. As this display is run over time, the sizes and shapes of the octahedrons will change as the underlying data change. The positions of the companies in the market space and in relation to each other will also change. All of this information can be quickly seen and understood by people because our visual sense is so well tuned to detect trends and make projections based on moving 3D images.

for each company. In the next period of time, a company can position itself anywhere within its "maneuverability sphere." The sphere is centered on the company's center point and its radius is calculated as:

$$R = (\text{Gross Profit} / \text{Total Liabilities}) \times \text{Total Assets}$$

The maneuverability sphere equation is an adaptation of the energy-maneuverability equation devised by John Boyd to describe the potential maneuverability of an airplane. His equation is:

$$P = ((\text{Thrust-Drag}) / \text{Weight}) \times \text{Velocity}$$

In adapting Boyd's energy-maneuverability equation to describe a company, we are making some assumptions or drawing analogies between airplanes and companies. We are saying that a company's sales revenue is analogous to the thrust of an airplane's engine and that cost of sales is similar to drag on an airplane. Therefore, gross profit is similar to thrust minus drag. We go on to assume that a company's total liabilities are analogous to an airplane's weight and that total assets are similar to velocity.

This example is just a beginning. There are many other assumptions and analogies that need to be explored. Some assumptions and analogies will prove to be invalid, and others will provide amazing insights into the workings of companies and business units within companies as they operate in the real-time world. The key is that we begin to use this type of technique as the way to display and make sense of real-time data. The thought leader interview in Chapter 6 shows how people are already using virtual reality technology to build and operate these kinds of moving 3D environments. (See Exhibit 5.4.)

ENDNOTES

1. Robert Coram, *Boyd, The Fighter Pilot Who Changed the Art of War* (Boston, New York, London: Little, Brown and Company, 2002).
2. Ibid., p. 135.
3. Material on the OODA Loop can be found on the Internet and in several books. Two authoritative Web sites are *www.belisarius.com* and *www.d-n-i.net*. Robert Coram's book (see note 1) is also a good source.
4. Sun Tzu, *The Art of War,* Thomas Cleary, translator (Boston: Shambhala Publications, Inc., 1988), p. 91.
5. A thoughtful book that expands on the analogies between business and war is written by Mark McNeilly, *Sun Tzu and the Art of Business* (New York: Oxford University Press, 1996).
6. Ibid., p. 95.
7. U.S. Marine Corps, *Warfighting* (New York: Currency/Doubleday, 1989).

8. Ibid., p. 79.
9. Ibid., p. 67.
10. Ibid., p. 68.
11. General George S. Patton Jr., "Notes on Combat Armored Divisions" (1944), *http://www.pattonhq.com/textfiles/divnotes.html*.
12. Stafford Beer, *Brain of the Firm* (New York: John Wiley & Sons, 1981), p. 195.
13. Vivek Ranadive, *The Power of Now: How Winning Companies Sense & Respond to Change Using Real-Time Technology* (New York: McGraw-Hill, 1999), p. 185.

CHAPTER 6

Resourceful Use of Information Technology

It is essentially true that information technology (IT) has become a commodity and that it offers no competitive advantage in and of itself. But then this is true of most things. Money itself is the ultimate commodity. Merely having money or IT is not necessarily an advantage. The advantage comes from how you use it and what you create with it.

Our economy is in a period of major structural change. Whole industries are changing and markets are placing value in new areas. Companies need to keep in touch with what their markets value and find ways to deliver goods and services in a cost-effective manner.

Economic necessity is the mother of business invention. Successful companies are those that learn to constantly improve their operations as well as deliver new products and services to their customers—this is the agile real-time company. To do this requires enhancements to existing information systems and development of new systems. This chapter provides a framework for understanding how to use technology to support the real-time enterprise.

USING TECHNOLOGY TO SUPPORT THE REAL-TIME ENTERPRISE

There is a bewildering array of three-letter acronyms being generated by IT vendors and consultants. New acronyms come out every year. They come and go so fast now that it is hard to make sense of them any more. This flood of acronyms is driven by IT vendors attempting to differentiate their products from those of their competitors and to call attention to themselves. Incremental product enhancements and minor changes are billed as entirely new inventions.

There is a constant effort to deliver the next "insanely great new thing" or the next "killer app" in the IT industry. Vendors and consultants had great success in the 1990s by creating surges of interest around some new concept or product. Great surges of interest were created around things such as client/server computing, object-oriented design, enterprise resource planning (ERP), customer relationship management (CRM), and e-commerce of all sorts.

Billions of dollars of products and services were sold to companies who became interested in those things. These surges of interest and spending reached a crescendo in 2000. IT spending has since been curtailed in many companies because it became evident that IT products alone do not produce value.

The only way business value is created by IT products is for them to be used by people in a company to either cut costs or increase revenues. For this to happen, business and technical people need to find a clear way to communicate with each other about the business requirements of a situation and how technology can be used to help. The four steps of the OODA Loop (observe–orient–decide–act) provide just such a way to communicate.

When describing a business problem or opportunity, people can discuss what the requirements are in the observe step, the orient step, the decide step, and the act step. IT products and services can be classified by their ability to meet requirements in one or more of these steps. As people become familiar with the product offerings in each category, they can sketch out IT solutions to their business needs by creating combinations of appropriate products and services.

By using the four steps of the OODA Loop to classify IT offerings, we reduce the confusion caused by the constant introduction of new three-letter acronyms. Using this classification, we start to make sense of the ever-changing array of technology products. Instead of discussing individual products as they come and go, we can instead see how these products fit into a much more stable and meaningful business framework.

Observe: Data Collection, Transmission, and Storage

IT products that fall in this category are the hardware and software used to collect data, send data from one location to another, and store data. This category contains IT products such as point-of-sale (POS) systems and order entry systems in which data is manually typed in. Other data collection technologies are cell phones, video cameras, fax machines, bar code scanners, and sensors that can detect properties such as motion, heat, sound, electromagnetic radiation, and so on.

Sensors are becoming a very powerful way to observe an environment and collect data. One sensor technology that is getting a lot of attention is radio frequency identification (RFID) tags. RFID is the next generation of bar-coding technology. Where bar codes have to be seen and optically scanned, RFID tags now broadcast their data to sensors equipped with radio receivers. RFID tags are being attached to the products that move through a company's supply chain. Without requiring any human intervention, scanners read the RFID tags on pallets and individual items as they move into and out of warehouses, trucks, and stores. This makes tracking of products and calculation of inventory levels throughout a supply chain now possible in real time.

Another sensor technology that is starting to be employed in a variety of applications is called "smart dust." This refers to a wireless network of very tiny sensors. They are simply scattered over an area the way one would toss out a handful of sand. The tiny sensors can be configured to sense whatever is of interest—the presence of certain chemical compounds, or heat, sound, motion, and so on. The sensors then establish a communication network between themselves and begin sending the data they collect to some remote location.

In the business world a class of systems called business process management (BPM) systems or business activity monitoring (BAM) systems are taking hold. These systems tap into the data stream generated by existing transaction processing systems such as purchasing, order entry, inventory management, or accounts receivable. BPM or BAM systems monitor the operating status of these systems. They alert people when slowdowns occur, when certain predefined events occur, and when system performance goes outside of predefined parameters.

The observe category also contains technology for data transmission such as the Internet, electronic data interchange (EDI), local area networks and wide area networks (LANs and WANs), and wireless data transmission. The spread of high-speed data transmission technology known as broadband technology is replacing the older and slower dial-up telecommunication modes of data transmission. It is getting less expensive all the time to collect and transmit huge amounts of data.

The technology in the observe category generates an enormous amount of data, and this amount is growing every year. To meet the needs of storing, retrieving, and securing this data, new products are being introduced that store and encrypt this data. IT vendors are delivering technology such as storage area networks (SANs) and network attached storage (NAS) that offers the high-capacity storage needed to handle huge volumes of data.

Orient: Turning Data into Information

As we saw in Chapter 5, orientation is at the heart of the OODA process. It is where raw data gets turned into information. Collecting data is the easy part. Figuring out what to make of it and what to do with it is the hard part. Data is turned into information by first spotting the data that contains "unpredictable news" or exceptions to the norm and then displaying it in ways that are meaningful and quickly understandable by the people who need the information to do their jobs. There are many different ways to turn data into information, depending on the needs and preferences of the people who use it.

Business intelligence (BI) is the term often used to describe the technology that displays information to people in an organization. This technology involves collecting data from transaction-processing systems in a company and putting it in specially designed databases known as data warehouses or data marts. A process known as *extract, transform, and load* (ETL) is what takes data from different transaction systems and puts it into a data warehouse.

Once in a data warehouse, data is accessed and displayed by people using what is called a *portal*. A portal uses an Internet Web browser to access data and display it in a format that is defined by people according to their own individual needs and preferences. Portals can also display data obtained directly from transaction processing systems or from BPM or BAM systems.

Portals display messages or alerts received from BPM or BAM systems when the performance of certain business processes goes outside of predefined parameters. Portals allow people to define the information they want to see and define the rules that indicate when the performance of a given business process is starting to deteriorate.

Customized portal displays are called *dashboards* because they allow people to see at a glance the information that is important to them. Dashboards alert people to the exceptions in normal business processes that need their attention and a quick response.

Many IT vendors produce portal and dashboard technologies that consolidate data from different systems and data warehouses. This technology provides appropriate business intelligence to people who can use it on a daily or hourly basis. It lets them see what is going on in the business operations for which they are responsible. Learning to use portals is the first step for people to take as they begin to understand how to operate and manage a real-time enterprise. (See Exhibit 6.1.)

Decide: Weighing Alternatives and Making Choices

The process of deciding what to do once you have been alerted to a problem is something that is aided by software that evaluates the effectiveness of possible responses. This ranges from analysis of different options using a spreadsheet to the testing of different courses of action using sophisticated simulation software.

Simulation software is a category that is growing rapidly. There is software to simulate the flow of materials through a factory or a supply chain. People can simulate different factory designs and supply chain configurations to see which is the most efficient. There is software to simulate the performance of a portfolio of stocks. There is software to simulate the financial performance of a company under different market conditions and organizational structures. The list goes on.

It is important to understand that the simulation software can run its simulations using the very same stream of real-time data captured by the systems that an organization uses to observe its environment. When this real-time data goes through the systems that a company uses for orientation, those systems spot exceptions and note where operating results are outside of desired

EXHIBIT 6.1   A SAMPLE PERSONAL DASHBOARD

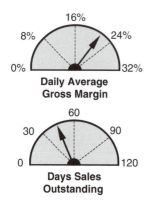

Daily Average
Gross Margin

Days Sales
Outstanding

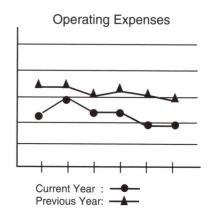

Operating Expenses

Current Year : ●
Previous Year: ▲

Gross Profit

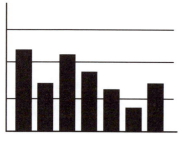

Gross Profit Amount by Location

Key Metrics

	MTD	QTD	YTD
Revenue	136	436	1,234
Gross Profit %	18	19.5	20.2
Units Sold	2,334	6,455	12.458
Avg Rev / Order	52.26	51.30	50.56
Customer Count	1,345	1,289	1,355

Each person using a dashboard display can customize it to their liking. Data can be displayed as line graphs, bar charts, tables, or dials. The exact display type and the numbers to be displayed are defined by the individual.

parameters. At that point, alerts are issued to people who need to respond. These people can often use simulation systems to try out different responses using the actual data that caused the alert in the first place. Simulations can identify effective responses before they are put into action. Running scenarios in a computer is often more cost effective and faster than trying things out in the real world.

Knowledge management (KM) or executive information systems (EISs) store and retrieve information from past experiences. Instances similar to a present situation can be retrieved and the results of past actions evaluated. These systems act as the institutional memory of an organization. Effective actions in similar circumstances, known as *best practices,* can be identified and used again. Just as importantly, ineffective actions can also be identified, and people can avoid repeating the same mistakes.

Act: Improve Existing Procedures or Create New Procedures

There are IT products and services to help companies act in every area one can think of. Application systems from stock trading to purchasing, from factory production scheduling to warehouse management exist to carry out the daily and hourly actions that company operations call for. All actions are either for the purpose of making existing processes as efficient and re-sponsive as possible or for creating new processes to respond to new de-velopments. IT products and services in the act category are designed to do one or the other of these things.

When evaluating products and systems to improve existing procedures, it is important to keep in mind the continuous improvement process de-fined by six sigma. These systems should produce a continuous stream of data that can be easily collected by business process management (BPM) or business activity management (BAM) systems to monitor day-to-day oper-ating efficiencies and produce alerts when performance levels stray outside of preset parameters. These systems are the control levers people use to op-erate their businesses so they should be easy to use and responsive to the most important needs of an operation.

Products and services designed to help companies create new processes and new ways of doing things are in great demand, and there are many of-ferings in this area. At present, the IT industry is much better at improving existing processes than at successfully creating new processes and systems. So it is important to understand that the failure rate is very high when try-ing to do new things.

Effective ways to manage risk are key to success. Products or services that call for a company to gamble large amounts of money in the hope that a big new system will pay off should be avoided. Betting the farm, so to speak, on high-stakes projects to build something new is a sure way to lose lots of money. In the three chapters that follow, we will go into some detail about how to successfully create new systems and procedures that the real-time enterprise needs. (See Exhibit 6.2.)

TOWARD A NEW IT STRATEGY

For most of the last 30 years, strategies for using IT usually consisted of making multimillion-dollar investments in whole new collections of hardware and software. Massive new systems were built from scratch or from extensive and expensive application software packages. The success rate of these endeavors has been modest, to put it politely. These kinds of strategies have run their course and are no longer viable ways to meet the needs of the real-time enterprise.

The real-time world is by definition a constantly changing world. Companies have tried to find answers to complex and fluid problems by installing standard application packages (ERP, CRM, supply chain management, etc.). This practice will only go so far. Companies that do this run the risk of lock-

EXHIBIT 6.2   IT PRODUCT CLASSIFICATION USING OODA LOOP

OBSERVE Data Collection, Transmission and Storage	ORIENT Turning Data into Information	DECIDE Weighing Alternatives and Making Choices	ACT Improve Existing Processes or Build New Ones
Point-of-sale systems	BI systems	Simulation systems	Existing systems
Order entry systems	Portals	Knowledge management	BPM and BAM systems
BPM and BAM systems	Dashboards	Spreadsheets	Web Services and SOA
Cell phones	BPM and BAM systems	etc.	New systems
Video cameras	EIS systems		etc.
Bar codes and scanners	etc.		
RFID tags and readers			
"Smart dust"			
etc.			

ing themselves into rigid, commodity IT systems that are also available to their competitors. Big software vendors then control the pace of systems change instead of the evolving demands of a company's own business situation.

The time is ripe for a strategy whose aim is to combine people and computers into systems in which the strengths of each are brought to bear. In a high-change, fast-paced world, it is best to use simple, robust technology to automate well-defined sequences of standardized business procedures and rely on people to handle the exceptions to these standard procedures. This can be summed up as "Automate the rote and repetitious work, and free up people to do the creative stuff."

By automating the mass of rote, routine, and repetitious work, companies get great cost efficiencies. By empowering people to handle all the nonroutine stuff, they become very responsive to unique customer needs. In his book *The Power of Now,* Vivek Ranadive expresses this idea as "achieving best efficiency. . . ."[1] It is this blend of efficiency and responsiveness that enables a company to outperform its competition. There are four main points to understand about this strategy:

1. Quickly build systems that are good, not perfect.
2. Let computers do the routine work.
3. Focus people on handling the exceptions.
4. Continuously adjust systems and processes based on experience.

Quickly Build Systems That Are Good, Not Perfect

There is an ongoing debate in many companies that hinges on the answer to the question, "Should we build it fast or build it good?" In this time of rapid change in technology and in business, the answer is to build it fast. That means to build it so that it is "good enough." Build computer systems that get the job done and resist the temptation to overengineer them or give them features to deal with every conceivable possibility no matter how rarely they may happen.

Companies need to maximize use of existing systems and add new IT products and systems in a very pragmatic way. What is needed is a continuous, incremental approach in which new computer systems are created from components of older systems and the pace of development can move with the pace of business change. This means developing new systems by leveraging the capabilities and features of existing systems. It can be done by building data links between existing computer systems and creating simple user interfaces (often using portals and dashboards) that blend together functions from existing systems.

There exists a collection of simple IT components or building blocks that can be combined in different ways and used with existing computer systems to create whole new systems. Some of those building blocks are:

- *ASCII flat files (also known as text files).* Every computer made in the last 20 years can read and write ASCII files, so it's a great way to exchange data between different systems.

- *File transfer protocol (FTP).* Sending ASCII files over the Internet via FTP is the quickest, cheapest, and easiest way to move large amounts of data almost anywhere in the world.

- *E-mail or instant messaging (IM).* The quickest, cheapest, and easiest way to make contact with specific individuals almost anywhere in the world.

- *Batch processing.* Data is collected into a batch over some period of time and then imported into or exported from a computer. It is the oldest and simplest way to get data into or out of a computer. The batch cycle can be run every day, every hour, every 10 minutes . . . approaching real time.

- *Relational databases.* Over the last 15 years, the relational database has become the most common way to store data. It is easy to find data and get it into and out of these databases.

- *Web pages.* The look and feel of your typical Web page follows certain rules and ways of working. This has become the universal system interface that all computer users know how to operate.

- *Current-generation mobilephones.* The mobile phone is a device that is practically changing in our hands as we hold it. Millions of people allover the world have one, and they are now capable of sending and receiving voice, video, and data communications. These devices also allow their users to access the Internet, surf the Web, and send and receive e-mail. The humble mobile phone is a very handy interface between people and all sorts of computer and communications systems.

Most companies do not need to be anywhere close to the leading edge in their use of technology. It is far more important to use relatively simple technology in an excellent way. Excellence of use is what produces the results that businesses want, not the technology itself.

Let Computers Do the Routine Work

Use computers to do what they do best. Let them handle the day-in, day-out, repetitive processing of routine data related to basic transactions such as purchase orders, invoices, account balances, order status, address changes, and the like. Wherever there are people doing routine data entry or repetitious work of any sort, this is an opportunity to automate. Computers do this sort of work much better, faster, and cheaper.

Many computer systems are unnecessarily complex and expensive because they attempt to handle every possible situation that could arise. Instead, focus computer systems on processing the great majority of routine transactions that follow relatively simple rules. Automate the handling of only a small set of well-defined errors. Build high-volume and technically simple systems to support these routine transactions.

By doing this, you avoid the costs, the risks, and the delays inherent in building complex computer systems. IT complexity is not only expensive and risky, but once it is in place it is hard to change, so computer systems and the business processes they support become rigid. They rob companies of the flexibility they need to evolve as their markets change.

Focus People on Handling the Exceptions

The reason that companies can build simple computer systems is that they can use people to handle all of the complexity that these systems cannot handle. If the status of any transaction is such that it does not conform to a basic set of rules contained in a standard processing system, then, by definition, that transaction is an exception. All the processing system needs to do in that case is trap the data related to the transaction and alert an appropriate person to handle this exception. The person will take over from there and the computer system can return to processing the vast bulk of routine transactions that drive the business.

People who handle exceptions will either be able to correct the data so that it fits back into a standard process or they will take care of those transactions themselves from start to finish. They will have time to do this because they won't be bogged down and worn out doing the routine stuff.

Since exception handling is nonroutine, it is interesting. It involves thinking, communicating with others, and problem solving. People like doing this kind of work. It's fun. The human brain has been evolving for the last 200,000 years to do just this. And because the work is fun and interesting, people will do a good job and they will learn and continue to get better at it.

Effective exception handling is what creates value in the real-time enterprise. As products and services become commodities in their markets, their production and delivery must be standardized and automated in order to keep costs down. It is in the exceptions to the standard commodity transactions that companies will find opportunities to realize increased profits.

Continually Adjust Systems and Processes Based on Experience

An exception to a standard business process is due to either an error in the data related to the transaction or to a new type of transaction that the standard process is not equipped to handle. Regardless of the cause of the exception, there is a profit opportunity to be had if an organization can respond effectively.

If the exception is because of an error in the data, then people need to get involved in finding and eliminating the root cause of the error. Every time a root cause can be removed, it makes the process that much more efficient and thus more profitable.

If a new type of transaction is what caused the exception, then people need to find out what generated it. A new type of transaction is usually indicative of a development or a change that could be a new opportunity or a new threat. There is money to be made by responding effectively to new opportunities, and there is money to be saved by responding effectively to new threats.

The systems infrastructure of a real-time organization is continuously evolving. As people discover and eliminate root causes of transaction errors, transaction systems change accordingly. As people discover new opportunities and threats, they build new computer systems and procedures to deal with them. Those new systems that perform well are then added to the company's set of standard systems and procedures. In this way, old systems are gradually replaced with newer ones over time.

IT Infrastructure for the Agile Real-Time Organization

There is a body of thinking about the kind of IT infrastructure that a real-time company needs. This thinking is collected under the title of "service-oriented architecture" or SOA (another three-letter acronym). SOA is concerned with creating an IT infrastructure that will support the IT strategy previously discussed. It enables a company to first integrate the workings of its different internal systems and then to interconnect its systems with those of other companies with which it wishes to collaborate.

The techniques of designing SOA are evolving rapidly, and, at the same time, it is fair to say that these techniques are heavily based on the use of two technologies—XML and Web Services.[2] These two technologies will increasingly allow companies to recombine parts of their existing IT infrastructures to create new systems. They also allow companies to easily exchange data and coordinate activities with other companies with which they want to do business.

XML

This is a software technology that grew up during the last years of the 1990s. It stands for extensible markup language and it evolved from hypertext markup language (HTML). HTML is the language used to build all original Internet Web sites. As Internet Web pages evolved beyond static online documents and their content became fluid and started to change frequently, XML was created to dynamically define and manipulate data in Web-based applications.

XML allows systems developers to define data entities and also define and label the data attributes that make up these entities. For instance, a data entity could be "Customer" and its data attributes could be "First Name," "Last Name," "Address," "City," "State," "Zip Code," "Phone Number," and "Credit Limit." This is expressed in XML as (you can read this quite easily—go ahead):

```
<Customer>
<First Name>Joseph</First Name>
<Last Name>Hughes</Last Name>
<Address>123 Main Street</Address>
<City>Des Moines</City>
<State>IA</State>
<Zip Code>40660</Zip Code>
<Phone Number>5159999999</Phone Number>
<Credit Limit>10000.00</Credit Limit>
</Customer>
```

Associated with this data entity definition there is an XML schema. The schema defines the type of data that is stored in each data attribute. In the case of the customer data entity, it will define the data in the first name, last name, and city attributes as being character data. It will define the data in the zip code attribute as being an integer number and the data in credit limit as being a two-place decimal number. And so on.

XML stores all data as ASCII text files. (Remember, the ASCII text file is a format that all computers can read and write.) Computer systems that access XML data import these text files and use the related XML schemas to translate the text file into the data types that they represent. XML can also contain instructions for how to display the data and instructions for how to respond to different user inputs. When programs send XML data to other programs, they translate their internal data types into XML text files and schemas. Therefore, any computer that can import and export ASCII text files and that has an XML interpreter to translate text into its own internal data types can use XML to send and receive data from any other system.

Web Services

This technology builds on the capabilities of XML to provide a standard way for different programs or computer systems to work together by sending messages to each other across a network such as the Internet. Web services define standards that programs should use to create messages in the form of XML documents. Web services standards define how the XML documents will specify which program is to receive a message sent by another program and how those programs are to interpret the data contained in the XML document.

Computer systems or programs that are equipped with Web services interfaces can receive standard XML messages from any other system or program on the network. They can translate the XML data in the message into a format understood by their internal programming language and database. They then perform operations on this data as requested in the XML message, translate the results back into an XML return message, and send that message back to the system that sent the original message.

XML and Web services are very useful for sending data from one program to another and for linking together parts of existing computer systems with new programs to create whole new systems. They are fast becoming basic IT building blocks and will be the technology of choice to build out much of the new IT infrastructure needed by real-time organizations. They combine efficient reuse of existing systems with the ability to quickly provide specific new system functionality to address new business needs that arise as markets evolve.

THOUGHT LEADER INTERVIEW

VIRTUAL REALITY BECOMES VERY PRACTICAL

Joy Monice Malnar is an associate professor in the School of Architecture of the University of Illinois at Urbana–Champaign. Over the last 20 years Joy has practiced and taught architecture. She worked with the prominent Chicago firm of Skidmore, Owings, and Merrill and taught at Mundelien College and Loyola University of Chicago before joining the faculty at the University of Illinois. She has also been a faculty fellow of the National Center for Supercomputing Applications. She is the coauthor of the recently published book *Sensory Design* and of an earlier book *The Interior Dimension: A Theoretical Approach to Enclosed Space*. She holds a master's degree in architecture from the University of Illinois at Chicago and is a licensed architect.

Joy has been collaborating with a small group of people at the National Center for Supercomputing Applications (NCSA) to create a virtual reality system that architects can use to do their work. "Sketching and modeling have been two methods used for centuries by architects to design," said Joy. Virtual reality requires architects to enter into a whole new relationship with their designs. "Now the two methods merge into a simultaneous act resulting in a full-size building model, which allows for a multisensory, full-body experience, instead of just our minds doing a best-guess interpretation based on drawings and small scale models."

Two of the people that Joy is collaborating with are William (Bill) Sherman and Alan Craig. They are computer scientists at NCSA and have coauthored the book *Understanding Virtual Reality*. Both have worked extensively in a virtual reality environment called the CAVE™. The CAVE was invented at the Electronic Visualization Laboratory at the University of Illinois at Chicago. Bill Sherman and Alan Craig participated in its development and now assist users and continue to further develop the technology. The CAVE is a 10-by-10-by-10-foot cube that people can walk into. Dynamic computer graphics images are projected on the wall in front, to each side, and on the floor. You don a pair of stereoscopic glasses and position trackers and suddenly you are in a 3D world. It is almost as if you are in the "holodeck" of the starship *Enterprise*. You can walk through virtual environments or you can use your control stick (called the wand) to fly you through them.

Using this advanced CAVE technology, Joy has been working with another associate to craft it to her needs. Kalev Leetaru is a student in the School of Engineering at the University and a student at the NCSA. Several years ago Kalev created a program called ShadowLight-Mirage that allows the creation and exploration of 3D environments (*http://shadow light.ncsa.uiuc.edu/*). Joy and her students have been using this program heavily to build and evaluate architecture in the CAVE. "Virtual reality has advanced architectural drawing to what I call full-body design," said Kalev. "By that I mean it lets architects actively experience their creations rather than just passively view them."[3] He is constantly enhancing the program and adding features that make it more user-friendly. "That's the real beauty of working with Joy and her students. I get this constant feedback and I get a sense of what the system looks like through their eyes. They guide me through the parts of the system interface that they like and don't like. I keep making it easier and more powerful for them to use."

Joy freely admits that she knows nothing about computers and programming. Her intention is not to learn about technology but to use what it can do to create a whole new way to teach and practice the design of our built environment. "I think virtual reality is more than just a tool. It is a way for us to learn to use capabilities of sense perception that been evolving for eons," she explained. "Using all these different sense perceptions lets the designer work on so many more levels than is possible with pencil and paper or with computer-aided design programs that are viewed on a flat computer screen.

"We don't use just our direct frontal vision; we also use our peripheral vision to process lots of data. Our eyes can pick up the subtlest patterns as we walk through an environment. It is often something caught out of the corner of our eye that alerts us to a change or to something interesting. Then add to this the use of sound. Sound tells us so much about things in our environment like where they are, how close they are, if they are moving, and so on." Joy explained that being able to handle and respond to all this sensory input makes a person a better designer. It also takes the design experience to a new level. "My students tell me that they actually work up a sweat—that they are physically tired after a two-hour session in the CAVE. I have to believe that working in the CAVE is healthier than sitting in front of a computer monitor—especially as the university's kinesiology department continues to conduct research establishing links between moderate exercise and our immune system and psychologist Arthur Kramer's research team using high-tech neuroimaging are finding that exercise increases the number of brain cells and neurons."

As Joy and I talked, Bill brought up a program that modeled the flow of water droplets in a wind tunnel. "Let's see what it's like to stand in the middle of this flow of water drops," Bill said to me. I put on my stereoscopic glasses and followed Bill into the CAVE. Using the wand he carried in his hand, he rotated the perspective and we moved through the tunnel until we were standing near the back watching hundreds of virtual water droplets seemingly flow through us and swirl down the length of the wind tunnel. Individual droplets changed colors as they cooled and their temperatures dropped. As an executive who works for a distribution company, I thought to myself, "These droplets could just as well be shipments of product moving through a supply chain—wow, talk about 'end-to-end visibility' in a supply chain. . . ."

The water droplets got me going. I described my flyby effect to Joy and Kalev (see Chapter 5, Executive Insight section). I explained how the three dimensions of the environment would be defined by data such as cost of sales, gross profit, and revenue. I described how each individual company in that environment would be represented as an octahedron whose exact dimensions would be determined by values such as the company's total assets, net tangible assets, and total liabilities. And then I told them that if we fed a stream of financial data through this display, it would make the company octahedrons move through the space and change their shapes as they moved. Joy assured me that I was describing a space that an architect can relate to and that some of her students had even designed abstract spaces that were somewhat similar to mine.

Kalev said he'd help me use the ShadowLight-Mirage software to start building this environment I described. Once again, I donned my stereoscopic glasses and entered the CAVE. Kalev showed me how to use the wand to draw in space. I began creating 3D objects. He showed me how to call up command menus that seemed to float in space in front of me (see Exhibits 6.3 and 6.4). I used these menus to copy objects, size them, and add color and texture. When I wanted to take a closer look at an object I reached out and touched it with the wand and brought it up close to my face. I was catching on fast. My mind raced with the possibilities.

The CAVE facility is located on campus in the building of the Beckman Institute for Advanced Science and Technology. From the CAVE, we took the elevator down to the facility of another researcher, Hank Kaczmarski, Director of the Integrated Systems Lab at the Beckman Institute. He and some colleagues have been building an even more advanced 3D environment called the Cube. You walk in and it surrounds you on six sides—all four walls plus ceiling and floor. Joy and Hank and I stepped into the Cube and Hank called up a series of programs that displayed everything from the spread of suburban development across the southern Illinois landscape to the movement of molecules in a cloud of gas. In each of these programs, we were in the middle of the display. We moved and flew about to get different perspectives. It was exhilarating to interact with the data this way.

The computer technology used to power the Cube is considerably less expensive than the technology used a mere handful years ago to create the CAVE. When the CAVE was built, it needed Silicon Graphics® computers to provide the necessary graphics. The Cube uses standard Intel-based servers running either Windows or Linux. The 3D animation software that powers the Cube was paid for by grant money that called for the software to be in the public domain. It can be downloaded for free. Hank and his colleagues can be contracted to help set it up. This is truly resourceful use of IT, and it is a taste of what is to come.

EXHIBIT 6.3   NAVIGATING IN 3D: EXAMPLE 1

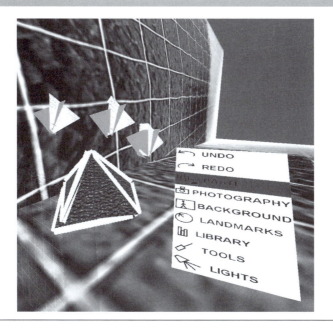

EXHIBIT 6.4   NAVIGATING IN 3D: EXAMPLE 2

ENDNOTES

1. Vivek Ranadive, *The Power of Now: How Winning Companies Sense and Respond to Change Using Real-Time Technology* (New York: McGraw-Hill, 1999), p. 99.
2. A clear and detailed description of XML and web services technology is given by Eric Newcomer, *Understanding Web Services* (Boston, MA: Addison Wesley, 2002).
3. Kalev Leetaru and Emma Smith, "Architectural Design in Immersive Virtual Reality," *http://shadowlight.ncsa.uiuc.edu/*.

CHAPTER 7

The Challenge of
System Building

This chapter begins our discussion of the process for building new systems. As we saw earlier, when the agile business decides to act, that means it will either improve an existing operation or create something new, and the decision to create something new means building new systems. The building of the real-time enterprise itself calls for a lot of activity in the "create something new" category. Success in the real-time world calls for systems that empower people to be effective players in a new way of doing business.

To begin with, in order for any system development project to succeed there must be a qualified person in charge of leading the project. People in this role are part architect—they must design a system that meets the demands of a particular situation—and part general contractor—they must then get the system built. This is the person who starts with the project and sees it all the way through. I'll call this person the *system builder.* The second requirement for success is that there be an appropriate project team or group of project teams assigned to the project. Project teams should consist of two to seven people with the proper mix of skills as called for by the project they are working on. There are six basic techniques that every system development team uses. Depending on the specific circumstances that surround a given project, teams will use some of these techniques more intensively than others. I call these six techniques the *core techniques.* We will look at what these techniques are later in this chapter.

WHAT ORGANIZATIONS NEED FROM INFORMATION TECHNOLOGY

Organizations expect two things from their information technology (IT) groups. The first is efficient and reliable operation of existing systems. The second is effective development of new systems to support business growth and change.

The IT profession does the first thing very well—people succeed most of the time. Existing systems, from telephone systems to e-mail to a company's order entry and accounting systems, operate so reliably that they are taken for granted. It takes a lot of hard work and skillful operations to make this happen, and we do it well.

The second thing is done very badly—most system development projects are failures. Depending on which survey you read and how you define success, projects fail anywhere from 50% to 80% of the time.[1] A major reason for this is the lack of a qualified system builder and project teams that are not trained in the use of the core techniques. Success rates will rise in a big way if executive sponsors of a project make sure there is a qualified system builder in charge. Then the system builder needs to put together project teams that are well trained in the core techniques.

THE SYSTEM BUILDER

The system builder is the bridge between business and technology. People in this role exist to design and deliver systems that make their organizations more efficient and better equipped to succeed. The skill and competence of the system builder goes a long way to determining the success or failure of the project.

If this person does not exist or is not up to the challenge, the project will devolve into a "management by committee" boondoggle, with the inevitable cost overruns and failure that result from that dynamic. One of the most important tasks facing the senior business executive who sponsors a system development project is to see to it that a capable system builder is found to lead the project.

This may be a person who comes up through the technical ranks, or sometimes this person comes up through the business side. Either way, over a period of years this person learns and practices the use of the core techniques. The system builder must also understand business and the specific business issues that a given system will address and must speak both the language of business and the language of technology.

This person is a lively student of technology and an active participant in the great game of business. The system builder must always be looking for ways to apply technology to make business more competitive or more profitable. The profession of system building is essentially composed of two activities: (1) designing systems and (2) leading projects to build systems.

Designing Systems

In my experience over the last 20-plus years, I have come up with a short list of five capabilities or skills that the system builder must have in order to be any good at designing systems. There are certainly other skills, but without these five as a foundation, a person cannot excel at the design process:

1. Understand the business operation.
2. Create an inclusive process.
3. Tolerate not knowing.
4. Look for the simple underlying patterns.
5. Use simple combinations of technology and process.

Understand the Business Operation   The design of an effective system begins with an understanding of the business landscape and how it is evolving. The system builder develops ongoing relationships with the people who work in different areas of the business and talks with them about what they see, what they need, and what the competition is doing.

The people who will actually use a new system already know many, if not most, of the features and capabilities they need. The trick here is to fit these ideas together in such as way as to produce an understandable and useful system. One hallmark of a well-designed system is that the people it is designed for learn to use it quickly and like it because many of the system features came from their own ideas.

It is essential for the system builder to have an appreciation of the business operation that the system is designed to improve. The system builder must understand the basic concepts or rules that guide the business operation, what the cost factors are, and how the operation fits into the overall business activity of the organization. A system is a means to an end, not an end in itself. Improvement of business operations is always the end to which a system is built.

If the system builder does not already have personal experience in the business operation that a system is being designed for, then it is a good idea to spend time observing and working alongside the people who currently perform this work. If people believe that the system builder wants to learn what they do and has an open mind about how to help them, they will take the time and make the effort to educate this person and share their ideas for improvement. It is through this experience that the system builder will begin to formulate the broad outlines of what the new system will look like.

Create an Inclusive Process   System builders must learn ways to deal effectively with complexity. They must consistently produce competent designs in the face of high complexity in both the business environment and the system technology. Complexity can be effectively dealt with if different people with the appropriate skills and experience are brought together in a collaborative process. The problem of complexity loses much of its power to intimidate and overwhelm if people work in groups instead of on their own.

The system builder must be skilled at orchestrating this collaborative process. Sally Helgesen, in her book *The Web of Inclusion,* says this requires people "who feel comfortable being in the center of things rather than at the top, who prefer building consensus to issuing orders. . . ."[2] The system builder must be able to elicit the ideas and insights of the full range of people—business, technical, managerial, sales, and the like—who will be affected by the system being designed.

The notion that any single person can form a complete picture of the problem and the possible options and can design the solution system all by him- or herself is a romantic myth from a much simpler time. By organizing an inclusive design process that includes all relevant parties, the system builder is able to deliver system solutions that are consistently competent and sometimes even brilliant.[3]

Tolerate Not Knowing   Becoming immersed in the details is a good thing. Do not rush to judgment. It is an act of discipline (and sometimes courage) to keep an open mind while analyzing the situation and investigating various possible solutions. The human mind wants to know—it likes answers, so it is natural to seize on the first or second idea that comes along. When this happens, the mind becomes closed and cannot see anything that does not then support its preconceived notions. Because of the complexity of the situations for which systems are being designed, it is unlikely that a good solution will be in the first or even the second idea that comes along.

The system builder first coordinates the analysis of the situation and then displays the results of that analysis in a form that is easily understood and absorbed by all the people involved in the design process. This is usually a graphic form using charts, diagrams, tables, and lists. The designer then facilitates a process with the design team wherein they create as many different solutions as time will allow.

In the words of Christopher Alexander, an influential architectural designer, "Design is the process of organizing form under a complex variety of constraints."[4] The experienced designer will allow the creative tension to build by not falling in love with an initial design and continuing to generate more different designs for possible solution systems. These different initial designs will provide the raw material and ideas from which the final design emerges.

Look for the Simple, Underlying Patterns   This is the creative leap where analysis gives way to synthesis and the design emerges. At first, you are assailed by the surface complexity of the situation and all the available technology. If you are able to tolerate ambiguity and work through an analysis of the situation and generate a range of possible solutions, then some profoundly simple and useful insights will start to emerge.

This kind of creative insight seems to emerge from what we call the subconscious mind. Facts and ideas are generated by the conscious mind and fed to the subconscious mind for further processing. You will know when these useful insights arrive because they will have a very obvious or "of course" quality about them. You will say, "Why didn't we see that a month ago? . . ." But neither you nor anyone else on the project team saw that when you began your analysis. All good designs are based on these profoundly simple and useful insights.

Since most of us are not geniuses, there really are simple underlying patterns to what we do or we would not be able to do what we do day after day. The complexity is generated by countless variations on a simple, underlying pattern or set of patterns. In his book *The Fifth Discipline,* Peter Senge states that good system designs must be based on an understanding of these simple patterns that shape the work we do.[5]

Once these workflow patterns are revealed, the system designer can design a system that fits closely to these patterns. A system so designed will be both quickly understandable by the people who must use it and also inherently flexible enough to deal effectively with many of the possible variations of these workflow patterns that arise.

Use Simple Combinations of Technology and Process   The system builder is also a student of technology and how technology is evolving. Computing and communications technology is the material that the system builder uses to create solutions to business needs. The system builder must have a feel for the strengths and weaknesses of the main hardware, software, and operating system platforms that are available.

The system builder must know of situations in which a certain technology worked well and those in which it did not. With the rate of change in the technology field today, keeping up with new developments is a continuous process. Develop a network of contacts with people who work with key technologies and talk with them about their experiences. Read industry magazines and attend conferences and trade shows.

Strive to create technical system designs that display an "elegant simplicity." Use as few technology components as possible while at the same time using each component for its strengths. Combine technology components in such a way that the strengths of each component complement each other to provide the operating and performance features that are needed in the system. Where possible, take advantage of existing system infrastructure that has proven over time to be stable and responsive.

Beware of the cleverness trap. We humans like to show our intelligence by engaging in displays of mind-boggling detail. If the details of a particular design seem overwhelming, then the design is probably too complex—too clever. This complexity will haunt the project as people try to build the system. It is normal in the design process for the first several designs to be too clever and complex. Work through this and look for the elegantly simple design to emerge. It will.

Leading Projects

The system builder is by necessity a leader more than a manager. This person is part visionary, in order to create and sell the ideas of a new system, and part politician, in order to do the negotiations and design changes required to secure the support of all the people needed to make the system a success. Through it all, the system builder is the focused, driving force who is totally committed to getting the work done and making the system a reality.

It is important to note that leadership will be more in demand than management skills. A leader creates something new, whereas a manager sees to the efficient running of something that already exists. Both are necessary. The important thing here is not to confuse the two. Confusion in this area has led to more than one disaster. Building systems is a process of creating something new, and leaders—not managers—are needed for the job.

I will summarize here what I have found to be the most important skills for the leadership of system development projects:[6]

- Be an effective communicator and negotiator.
- Set high standards and great expectations.
- Delegate, delegate, delegate.
- Be available.
- Be decisive.
- Act with energy and focus.

Be an Effective Communicator and Negotiator   The system builder as designer must create a compelling system vision. The system builder as leader must then share this vision with others in a way that attracts supporters and motivates them to action. The leader must be able to explain the system and its benefits to strangers at a cocktail party. If only technical people or industry insiders can understand the explanation then the communication is not effective. In addition to explaining the vision, the leader must also be able to clearly show how the project will progress from vision to reality. The progress must be broken down into a simple set of believable milestones that illustrate the sequence of activities that will build the system.

Good leaders have to find ways to use the talents they have to effectively communicate their message and negotiate for support of their ideas. They do not need to be great public speakers or to have outgoing personalities. They do need to continuously search for ways that work for them to communicate with their constituency. Informal meetings one-on-one or with small groups of people are always very effective. The use of simple diagrams to illustrate the key concepts of a system is also effective. From time to time they should work with a qualified coach to improve their presentation and communication skills.

Set High Standards and Great Expectations   Good leaders always appeal to the longings and desires of their followers. People want to participate in a process or project that they believe will improve their skills and bring rewards such as recognition and money. The leader sets standards of performance that people will be proud to live up to. However, setting high standards alone is not enough. People do not like to fail, so if they do not believe that they can meet the high standards, they will not step forward. Leaders see to it that their people get the training and support they need to meet the high standards.

Daniel Burnham, the great Chicago architect who designed some of the first skyscrapers and the lakefront parks and boulevards of Chicago, said, "Make no small plans for they fail to stir men's souls." Define project goals that create great expectations. Go for goals that provide big gains. This is what will generate the enthusiasm and commitment needed to focus people's efforts on reaching these goals.

Here again, people do not like to fail, so for these great expectations to work, the leader must choose goals that are attainable. If the leader does not truly believe that the goals are attainable, then this doubt will communicate itself in a hundred small ways and the needed enthusiasm and commitment from the project team will not materialize.

Delegate, Delegate, Delegate   The leader sets the project goals and milestones and then gets out of the way. The leader delegates whole sections of the project to the qualified people who have been attracted to the project (if no qualified people have been attracted to the project, then stop the project).

All well-defined projects have a set of objectives or milestones that must be reached in order to finish the project. The project leader needs to delegate not just individual tasks but the entire set of tasks that leads to the achievement of a particular objective or milestone. If the project leader does not delegate effectively, there is no way the project can get done on time and on budget.

Delegation works best when people are delegated work that they have already expressed an interest in doing. They want to participate because they see the opportunity to increase their skills and gain rewards. People will rise to the challenges delegated to them when they clearly understand the overall project goal and their specific objectives.

People must also know that the project leader has confidence in their ability to do the work and that they would not have been given the work if there were doubts about their ability to get it done. Finally, people need to know that the project leader will be there to work with them and get them the resources they require to be successful. If people believe that they were delegated work and then left to fend for themselves, they will simply go into defensive mode and do nothing but make excuses.

Be Available   Delegating work does not mean delegating the leader's responsibility for the project. Leaders stay actively involved. One of the best ways to be actively involved is to listen intently to the people on the project when they bring up issues. In his book *Thriving on Chaos,* Tom Peters states, "Oddly enough, to listen, per se, is the single best 'tool' for empowering large numbers of others."[7]

In a very real sense, project leaders become the servants of the people on their projects. Their success is the leader's success, and if they are not successful, neither will the leader be successful. Leaders hold regular project meetings (usually weekly) that are a forum for honest discussion about progress and open-minded approaches to solving the problems that inevitably arise. In most cases people already have answers in mind for the problems they encounter or they can figure out answers quickly enough. What they need is to be able to openly discuss the issues and get the leader's thoughts. When leaders are available for this, their people will usually do the rest.

Be Decisive   In most system-building projects, the key leadership decisions involve how to allocate resources to achieve project objectives. As the project progresses, obstacles will arise that threaten the timely completion of critical tasks. When one of the teams on the project runs into an obstacle that demands the reallocation of resources or the redefinition of objectives, the project leader must become directly involved.

Difficult decisions have to be made with less-than-perfect information to keep the project moving. The Marine Corps speaks of the "70% solution," by which they mean an imperfect solution but one that can be made quickly and implemented with the resources at hand. Marines also limit the amount of time they put into analyzing the issues and developing plans. A competent decision made in a timely manner is better than a perfect decision made too late. When decisions are needed, leaders involve the appropriate people and set deadlines. They do the best analysis within the time available, make decisions, and move on.

If the leader does not get involved and make important decisions in a timely manner, the project will lose its momentum and eventually come to a standstill. Often, a consensus will emerge when the project leader involves the affected people in an analysis of the problem. However, if no consensus emerges, it is the leader's place to make the decision. If the leader of the project is not willing to make the tough decisions, then no one else will either. This lack of decisiveness has caused many fine projects to devolve into "analysis paralysis" and aimless wandering.

Act with Energy and Focus   Leading a project really is like herding cats. It requires constant selling of the project and its benefits to all the affected parties. Leaders encourage, cajole, and assist the project teams to keep up their progress on the project. The leader needs to communicate, set high standards and expectations, delegate, be available, and be decisive. As William Fulmer, a Harvard Business School professor, put it, "Leaders have to convey an almost constant sense of urgency—this usually requires a high level of energy."[8]

The behavior and attitude of the system builder is the single most powerful force for creating an effective or, conversely, a dysfunctional project environment. Leaders lead by setting an example. They lead from the front. When necessary, they get involved in the details of tasks that require their input. The leader's presence and demeanor goes a long way toward keeping people motivated and on track. Exhibit 7.1 summarizes the skill sets needed by the system builder.

THE CORE TECHNIQUES

Just as the game of basketball has some basic techniques such as dribbling, passing, and shooting, so too does the game of developing information systems. The skill levels of IT project teams can be measured by their capabil-

EXHIBIT 7.1   SKILL SETS FOR THE SYSTEM BUILDER

DESIGN SKILLS	LEADERSHIP SKILLS
• Understand the business operation	• Be an effective communicator and negotiator
• Create an inclusive process	• Set high standards and great expectations
• Tolerate not knowing	• Delegate, delegate, delegate
• Look for the simple, underlying patterns	• Be available
• Use simple combinations of technology and process	• Be decisive
	• Act with energy and focus

ities in these techniques. By employing these techniques in combinations that are appropriate to different situations, a project team will always be able to produce competent—and sometimes even brilliant—results. The following six techniques are a simple yet comprehensive set of skills that can be taught and mastered by people involved in building systems:

1. Joint application design
2. Process mapping
3. Data modeling
4. System prototyping
5. Object-oriented design and programming
6. System test and rollout

Joint Application Design

The joint application design (JAD) technique enables the system builder to create an inclusive process that brings together the knowledge and insights of all the team members. The JAD techniques lay down a set of rules that govern how the team leader will lead, how the team members will interact, and how a problem will be approached. These rules stimulate the creative problem-solving abilities of the team and allow the team to generate a stream of ideas that then become the raw material from which the system design emerges.

JAD is a response to the overwhelming complexity of the design tasks that we are faced with in business today. No one person on his or her own or even a group of people individually analyzing parts of a problem can come up with competent or adequate system designs on a consistent basis. However, using the JAD techniques, project teams with the appropriate mix of business and technical people can come up with competent system designs every time.

Process Mapping

Process mapping is a set of techniques for identifying the work processes that occur in a company and the connections among these processes.[9] First, the highest-level processes are identified, and then subprocesses are identified within each high-level process (see Exhibit 3.3). The data inputs required by each process are defined and the source of the data is listed. The data outputs generated by each process are also defined, and the destinations of the data outputs are listed.

This technique creates a visual map of the tasks in the business processes and the data flows between them. Diagrams are created that show tasks and data flows that go into and out of each task. This visual diagram creates a common framework for business and technical people to discuss business issues and discover opportunities for process improvements. These visual diagrams are far more effective than written documents because they use graphic means to communicate a lot of information quickly and accurately. Exhibit 7.2 shows an example of a process-mapping diagram.

Data Modeling

The data model defines the things or entities about which data needs to be collected. The entities will usually be identified while using the business process decomposition technique. Entities such as customer, product, and invoice will be in the data flows between different business processes. The data model then defines the properties or attributes that must be known about an entity. For example, the entity called *customer* will have attributes such as customer number, name, address, and credit limit.

EXHIBIT 7.2   PROCESS MAP

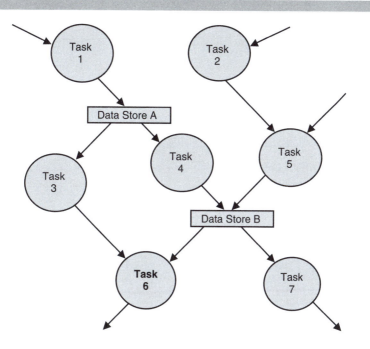

The process model shows the sequence of tasks in the workflow. It may also show places where data is stored.

This technique also produces a visual diagram called an entity relationship diagram (ERD). Like the process flow diagrams produced by the process-mapping technique, the ERDs provide another visual method for communicating a lot of information to the business and technical members of a project team. Everyone on a team can spot-check the entities on the diagram that they are familiar with to ensure accuracy. Exhibit 7.3 shows an example of an entity relationship diagram.

System Prototyping

There are two kinds of system prototyping. The first kind of system prototype is a model of the system's user interface. From the process-modeling technique the project team decides which processes will be fully automated, which processes will be a mix of human activity supported by a computer,

EXHIBIT 7.3   DATA MODEL—ENTITY RELATIONSHIP DIAGRAM

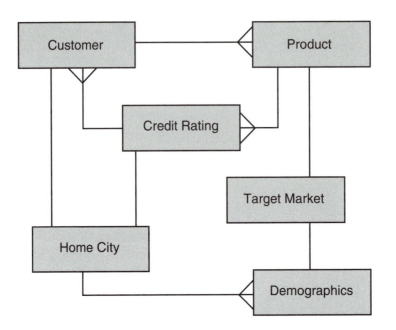

This sample data model shows that there are five entities that a certain business process needs to know about and how these entities relate to each other.

and which processes will be completely done by humans. From the data model, the team knows what data will need to be handled by the system. The system prototype of the user interface builds upon this knowledge to create the layout and sequence of computer screens that will support the processes where humans and computers interact. The user interface prototype also illustrates how the system user can navigate between screens, and it shows the layout of any printed output generated by the system. This prototype is created as an interactive slide show that is displayed on a computer screen and allows the system user to move from one screen to another via keyboard, mouse, or other commands. It shows the businesspeople what they will get when the new system is built. It is something tangible that people can work with, respond to, and make suggestions for improving.

The second kind of system prototype is an architectural prototype. It is put together using the hardware and software components that have been selected to build the system. It demonstrates how well these components will work together. The selected software is installed on the selected hardware. Links are established among the different software components, and data is passed back and forth under different conditions to get measurements of the hardware and software components' ability to work together and handle the expected number of users and volumes of data. It shows the technical people what issues they will face when they build the system. It allows people to verify that the technology they propose to use to build the system will work as advertised and that it will be able to meet the performance demands of the new system. Exhibit 7.4 illustrates the idea of the two types of system prototypes: the technical architecture and the user interface.

EXHIBIT 7.4   SYSTEM PROTOTYPES

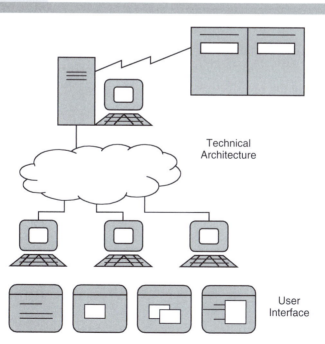

Technical Architecture

User Interface

The prototype of the system's technical architecture shows how the hardware and software components will work together.

Object-Oriented Design and Programming

Object-oriented design (OOD) and object-oriented programming (OOP) are the latest incarnation of a set of techniques that have been evolving for the last 30 years or so in the system-building profession. The purpose of these techniques is to enable the design and programming of software that is stable, reusable, easy to debug, and easy to modify.

The object-oriented techniques are analogous to the engineering techniques an electrical engineer uses when designing a piece of equipment such as a cellular phone. The cell phone will be specified as a collection of component parts. Many of these parts will be integrated circuit chips (IC chips) that are plugged into a motherboard. Each IC chip is defined by the inputs it accepts, the operations it performs, and the output it creates.

Objects are the software equivalent of the IC chip. A system is composed of interacting software objects just as a cell phone is composed of interacting IC chips. The much-talked-about technique of Web services is an example of OOP. Web services are composed of programs (objects) from existing systems that communicate with each other by sending inputs and receiving outputs over the Internet using agreed-upon XML formats.

Once the object-oriented design is done, the programming is a relatively straightforward process of writing code to meet the design specifications for each object. All the hard decisions about how the objects will operate and interact to drive the system are made in the object-oriented design. The choice of programming language will influence the design of the objects to some extent, but the object design is largely language independent.

The system builder can manage the programming effort very effectively by simply tracking the programming progress object by object. Generally, objects can be programmed in one to three days. They can be programmed in any order and can all be done in parallel if there are enough programmers available. In this way, new programmers can be added to speed up the programming process without causing confusion and loss of project control. Exhibit 7.5 illustrates a sample object model diagram.

System Test and Rollout

These techniques are used to test the system in a thorough and orderly manner so as to find and fix the bugs and then to introduce the system into production. These techniques allow the people on the project teams to first test

EXHIBIT 7.5   OBJECT MODEL

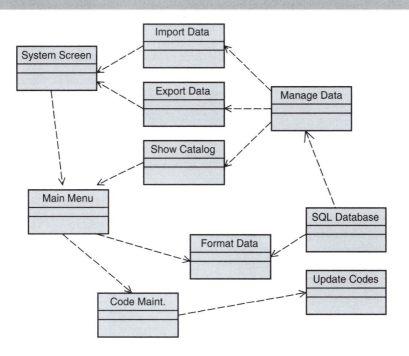

The object model shows the modules of program code—the objects—and how these objects interact with each other to drive the system.

each object individually, then to test the groups of objects used in each system function, and finally to test the entire system. The programmers who program each object first do unit testing on the object. When it passes the unit test, they check it into a system test environment. People who are familiar with the operations the system is designed to perform create test scripts, and these test scripts are used to put different parts of the system through its paces. The test scripts are written so as to exercise the different features of the system in a wide range of different usage scenarios. As more and more parts of the system come together in the test environment, eventually the entire system is assembled and tested.

Once the system has been tested in the test environment and bugs corrected, there is then a sequence to follow in rolling out the system. The first step is to roll out the system to a beta test or pilot group of people, who

EXHIBIT 7.6   THE CORE TECHNIQUES (SKILLS OF THE
GAME)

1. *Joint application design* for pooling the collective knowledge and ideas of a group of people working on a project so that an appropriate design is created

2. *Process mapping* for drawing out existing workflows and defining new workflows so that people can see and understand quickly

3. *Data modeling* for defining the kinds of data and volumes of data that a system will handle so that the database can be designed

4. *System prototyping* for building and testing a model of a system's user interface and its technical architecture to verify that it will meet performance requirements

5. *Object-oriented design and programming* for creating systems from combinations of predefined and reusable software components to enable efficient system construction and enhancements

6. *System testing and roll out* for debugging a system and training the people who will work with it so that the system is put into production quickly and used effectively

begin using the system to do their jobs. The pilot group will define a range of system modifications that fine-tune the operation of the system and improve the ease with which it can be used. Finally, the system rolls into production. Appropriate training always supports the roll into production so that the people who have to use the new system are not left to cope with the change entirely on their own. (See Exhibit 7.6.)

EXECUTIVE INSIGHT

BOOSTING CUSTOMER SERVICE AND SALES PRODUCTIVITY

Sunil Arora is the vice president of global e-commerce at Anixter International. Anixter is an international distributor of wire and cable and electrical communications products for handling data, voice, and video. In 2003 Anixter had revenues of $2.7 billion. Sunil started with Anixter as a business systems designer in their IT group. Since then he has learned the business through a series of jobs and promotions in his career with Anixter.

Last year he returned from Europe, where he was the VP of information services for Anixter Europe and Asia/Pacific. He was brought back to corporate headquarters to guide the roll out of the eAnixter suite of Web-based customer service and sales systems in North and South America. He had already introduced this system very successfully in Europe and Asia. Results there show that new sales and customer service procedures made possible by using the eAnixter system are a powerful combination for enhancing customer service and raising sales productivity.

"We surveyed sales offices and found that salespeople spent a significant amount of their time on postsales and customer service related activities," said Sunil. "At the same time, our customers were complaining that they could not always find Anixter sales reps when they needed to. We wanted to find ways to provide customers the service they needed when they needed it." He continued, "It was clear that the way to do this was to free up salespeople to spend more time selling. So we focused our eAnixter system on automating as much of the routine customer service and postsales work as possible. We also set up new procedures to use customer service reps for postsales work that can't be automated. A customer service person costs less than a salesperson so it's a lot more efficient that way. They report to the branch sales manager, and they are bonused on the profitability of their accounts, so they work closely with the salespeople and take good care of their customers. This was a significant change in our sales organization's way of doing business and, as expected, it took some time to implement."

The eAnixter system leverages existing legacy systems that have been used by sales people for many years. The legacy systems were given graphical, Web-based user interfaces and whole new applications were built to provide additional functionality. The new applications run on Web servers and the legacy systems run on mainframes, but they are all presented to the user through a Web browser using a unified set of screens that all have the same look and feel. Because of this approach, Anixter has been able to develop and deploy the system in a very cost-effective manner.

One of the key jobs necessary for success is to communicate the benefits of this new way of doing business. Sunil spends a lot of time getting the word out and demonstrating what eAnixter can do. It is a process of winning over supporters and then publicizing their successes with the system. This is what builds the momentum it takes to roll the system out.

"The system does not compete with our sales force," explained Sunil. "A customer can order online or through a sales person. The system also sends alerts to sales reps about orders placed by customers, any issues with those orders, order ship dates, and other relevant information. Four countries in Europe were the early adaptors of eAnixter. After a year our surveys showed that the most productive and highly paid sales people in those countries also had the most online business.

"I created a one-page report that measured use of eAnixter in each country. I sent this report to everyone from executive management to branch managers and sales reps. The report showed the number of new customer sign-ons and tracked usage measured as the percent of total customers that signed on at least once a month. We had a goal of 20 percent customer usage in Europe."

Sunil explained that some incentives were put in place to get salespeople to roll the system out to their customers. Salespeople set up product catalogs with the products and prices specific to each of their customers. Then the sales manager reviewed these catalogs before they are posted online. This allowed the salespersons to be more productive and to spend their time working with customers on the more complex and the more profitable orders. Thirty-five percent of Anixter Europe's business is now online. Sunil described some of the benefits that the business has experienced. "Average lines per order went up 50% and the average dollar amount per order is up 60%. It gives the customer a one-stop-shop convenience so they tend to order more."

Using eAnixter, the company has been able to support whole new ways of working with customers. They are able to offer a more customized mix of products and services to better meet peoples' needs. Sunil described some examples of this. For one customer, eAnixter allowed them to set up a bidding system where electrical contractors could submit bids for jobs that included Anixter products and the contractor's labor costs. Then the customer could review these bids online and send a work order to the contractor they selected.

On another occasion, Anixter set up a system that allowed a manufacturer of cable modems to take orders and send modems to people who signed up with certain Internet service providers. Anixter stocked and shipped the modems. Using eAnixter, the manufacturer could check online to see inventory levels of its modems at Anixter warehouses, where the modems where being shipped, and the number of modems that were being returned by customers.

"The better we can configure ourselves to fit the customer's needs, the more value we deliver to the customer," observed Sunil. "Implementing a new system like this requires people to learn a new way of working and come up with innovative approaches to use systems. It's a lot of work, but the rollout of eAnixter across Anixter's global business will have a huge effect on the company's competitiveness."

Endnotes

1. Standish Group, "The CHAOS Report" (West Yarmouth, MA, 1994–2001), *http://www.standishgroup.com/sample_research/index.php.*
2. Sally Helgesen, *The Web of Inclusion* (New York: Currency/Doubleday, 1995), p. 20.
3. This process of problem definition and resolution is well covered in an article by Richard Coyne and Adrian Snodgrass, "Problem Setting Within Prevalent Metaphors of Design," *Design Issues* 11, no. 2 (The Massachusetts Institute of Technology, Summer 1995).
4. Christopher Alexander, *Notes on the Synthesis of Form* (Cambridge, MA: Harvard University Press, 1971), p. 32.
5. Peter Senge, *The Fifth Discipline—The Art and Practice of the Learning Organization* (New York: Currency/Doubleday, 1990).
6. I am much influenced by the 11 characteristics of leadership in a complex environment presented by William Fulmer, *Shaping the Adaptive Organization* (New York: AMACOM, 2000), p. 228.
7. Tom Peters, *Thriving on Chaos* (New York: Alfred A. Knopf, 1987), p. 437.
8. William Fulmer, *Shaping the Adaptive Organization* (New York: AMACOM, 2000), p. 250.
9. A classic book on the technique of process mapping is written by Tom DeMarco, *Structured Analysis and System Specification* (Englewood Cliffs, NJ: Yourdon Press/P T R Prentice Hall, 1979).

CHAPTER 8

Developing Systems in Real Time

Companies in the real-time world are continuously adjusting and evolving their operations to respond to changes in their markets. To be successful in this process of continual response to change, companies rely on up-to-date information systems to help them make the right decisions. They also need new operations support systems to support the new business processes that they implement. So there is a continuous need to develop new systems.

In this chapter we will discuss the creation of strategy and the use of tactics as they relate to the development of information systems. The key to developing systems lies in learning how to respond effectively to the challenge of complexity. The define–design–build (DDB) approach to systems development provides a very potent way to deal with complexity.

APPLIED STRATEGY AND TACTICS FOR BUILDING INFORMATION SYSTEMS

Most of the time, terms such as *goals* and *objectives* or *strategy* and *tactics* are used interchangeably. The precise meaning of the words gets lost, and so the clarity of the thinking that these words can support is also lost. If we wish to gain any real value from the use of these words, then we owe it to ourselves to be very precise and clear in the way we use them. Otherwise, the words become trite phrases, macho imagery, or smokescreens for incompetence. The following list defines some key terms that will be used in our discussion.

- *Business vision.* This is a definition of the company's purpose, why it exists, what it aspires to. The business vision of the company is articulated by a set of goals that define what the company will strive for and where the company will invest its resources.

- *Goal (or mission).* A goal is a qualitative, but usually not quantitative, statement that describes a state of affairs or an accomplishment necessary for the business to become what it wants to become (the business vision). An example of a goal is "Strengthen and grow the national accounts sales program." Another example would be "Develop an e-business infrastructure to take advantage of market trends."

- *Objective (or milestone).* An objective must be quantitative. It is a statement that defines a specific, measurable achievement that is necessary to accomplish a goal. The strategy that a business uses to accomplish a goal defines the objectives that must be achieved along the way. The key is that an objective is measurable. Based on the facts, one can tell if an objective was achieved or not. An example of an objective is "Increase sales in the health care sector this year by 15%." Another example would be "Train all customer service people to use the new system this quarter." Objectives are the specific, measurable things that must be done to accomplish a goal or mission.

- *Strategy.* Strategy can be defined as simply "the use of *means* to achieve *ends.*" It is the art of using the means—business capabilities—available to a company to achieve its ends—its business goals. The degree to which a strategy is effective depends on a clear understanding of what is possible. Any strategy that calls for the use of means beyond the capability of a company is bound to fail. The purpose of strategy is to maximize the possibilities for the successful use of the means that are available. Strategies are used to accomplish goals or missions.

- *Tactics.* Tactics are the execution and control of actions needed to carry out the business strategies. Tactics are concerned with the effective coordination of people, process, and technology to achieve objectives that are defined by the business strategy. Tactics are the methods used to get things done. Tactics are used to achieve objectives.

- *Techniques.* A technique is a well-defined action or behavior producing a predefined result. A technique is a systematic procedure by which a task is accomplished. Combining techniques into useful sequences creates tactics.

- *Plan.* A plan is a nonrepetitive set of tasks that leads to the achievement of a new objective. A plan is not to be confused with an operating schedule, which is a repetitive set of tasks that are used to perpetuate an already existing state of affairs. The situation, the objectives defined, and the tactics being applied guide the creation of a plan. The sequence of tasks shown on the project plan reflects the tactics and techniques that are being used. (See Exhibit 8.1.)

EXHIBIT 8.1   APPLIED STRATEGY AND TACTICS

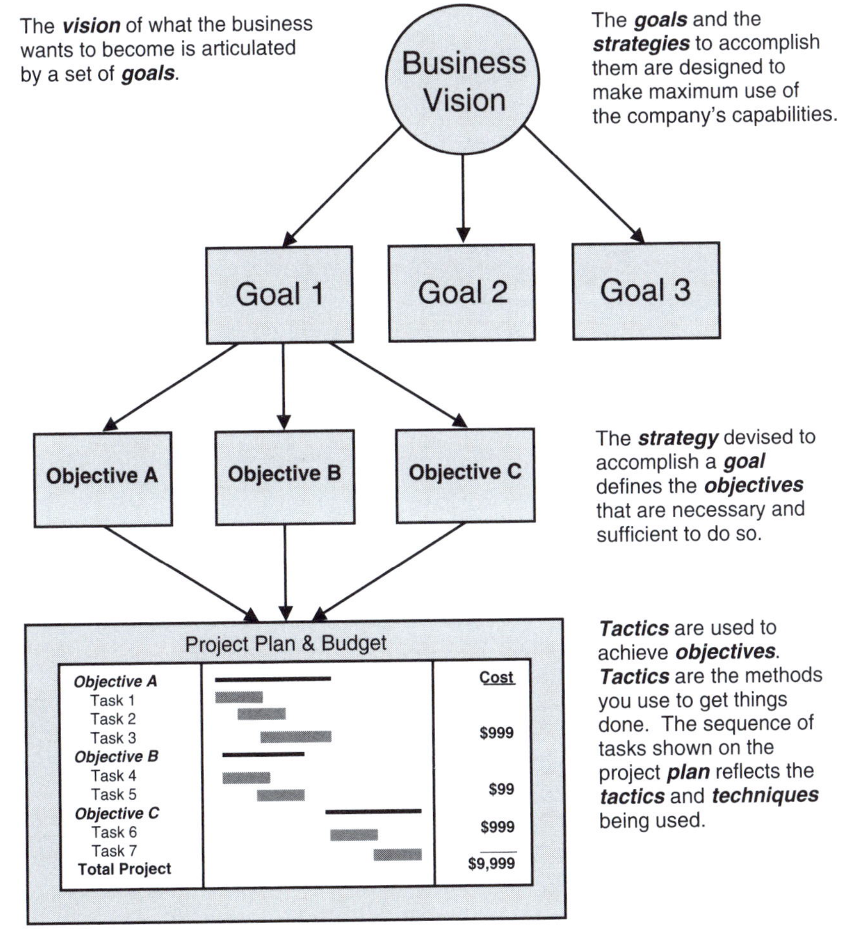

The **vision** of what the business wants to become is articulated by a set of **goals**.

Business Vision

The **goals** and the **strategies** to accomplish them are designed to make maximum use of the company's capabilities.

Goal 1   Goal 2   Goal 3

Objective A   Objective B   Objective C

The **strategy** devised to accomplish a **goal** defines the **objectives** that are necessary and sufficient to do so.

Project Plan & Budget

		Cost
Objective A		
Task 1		
Task 2		
Task 3		$999
Objective B		
Task 4		
Task 5		$99
Objective C		
Task 6		$999
Task 7		
Total Project		$9,999

Tactics are used to achieve **objectives**. **Tactics** are the methods you use to get things done. The sequence of tasks shown on the project **plan** reflects the **tactics** and **techniques** being used.

STRATEGIC GUIDELINES FOR DESIGNING SYSTEMS

Over the years, in my continuous efforts to summarize complex situations and find the simple underlying patterns, I have put together a short list of rules or strategic guidelines that I try to live by when designing and building computer systems. I have found that they guide me in the right direction when I use them and I have paid the price when I ignored them. There are five positive guidelines and two negative ones.[1]

Positive Guidelines

1. *Closely align systems projects with business goals.* For any systems development project to be a success it must directly support the organization to achieve one or more of its goals. No new system can be effective until you have first identified or created the business opportunity that will make the system worth building and no new system will bring any sustained benefit to your company unless it supports the efficient exploitation of the business opportunity it was built to address.

2. *Use systems to change the competitive landscape.* Ask yourself what seems impossible to do today, but if it could be done, would fundamentally change what your company does in a positive way. Put yourself in your customers' shoes. In the words of the Nordstrom motto, think of what would "surprise and delight" your customers. Look for opportunities to create a transformation or value shift in your market. Find ways to do things that provide dramatic cost savings or productivity increases. Place yourself in your competitors' shoes and think of what course you could take that would be the least likely to be foreseen or quickly countered or copied. As long as you are able to do something of value that your competitors cannot, you have an advantage.

3. *Leverage the strengths of existing systems.* When existing systems have proven over time to be stable and responsive, find ways to incorporate them into the design of new systems. The purpose of strategy is to best use the means available to the organization to accomplish its goal. The design of a system is the embodiment of the strategy being used. Build new systems on the strengths of older systems. That is

what nature does in the evolutionary process. New systems provide value only in so far as they provide new business capabilities. Time spent replacing old systems with new systems that do essentially the same things will not, as a general rule, provide enough value to justify the cost.[2]

4. *Use the simplest combination of technology and business procedures to achieve as many different objectives as possible.* A simple mix of technology and process that can achieve several different objectives increases the probability that these objectives can actually be achieved. This is because it reduces the complexity and the risk associated with the work and it spreads the cost across multiple objectives. Using a different technology or process to achieve each different project objective multiplies the cost and the complexity and reduces the overall probability of project success.

5. *Structure the design so as to provide flexibility in the development sequence used to create the system.* Break the system design into separate components or objectives and, as much as possible, run the work on individual objectives in parallel. Try not to make the achievement of one objective dependent on the prior achievement of another objective. In this way, delays in the work toward one objective will not impact the progress toward other objectives. Use people on the project who have skills that can be used to achieve a variety of different objectives. If you use the same technology to achieve several different objectives, it is much easier to shift people from one objective to another as needed because the skill sets used are the same. Your project plan should foresee and provide for an alternative plan in case of failure or delays in achieving objectives as scheduled. The design of the system you are building should allow you to cut some system features if needed and yet still be able to deliver solid value to the business.

Negative Guidelines

1. *Do not try to build a system whose complexity exceeds the organization's capabilities.* The beginning of wisdom is a sense of what is possible— "don't bite off more than you can chew." When defining business goals and the systems to reach those goals, aim for things that are within your reach. Set challenging goals but not hopeless goals. The

EXHIBIT 8.2 STRATEGIC GUIDELINES FOR DESIGNING SYSTEMS

POSITIVE

1. Closely align systems development projects with business goals and specific performance targets.

2. Use systems to change the business landscape.

3. Leverage the strengths of existing systems.

4. Use the simplest possible combination of technology and process to achieve the maximum number of objectives.

5. Structure the design so as to provide flexibility in the development sequence used to create the system.

NEGATIVE

1. Do not try to build a system whose complexity exceeds the organization's abilities to support it.

2. Do not renew a project using the same organization or the same system design after it has once failed.

---

people in your organization need to have confidence in themselves in order to rise to a challenge. Avoid exhausting their confidence in vain efforts to reach unrealistic goals.

2. *Do not renew a project using the same organizational approach or the same system design after it has once failed.* A mere reinforcement of effort or just trying harder is not a sufficient enough change to ensure the success of a project after it has once failed. People are usually demoralized after the first failure and will not rise to the challenge of doing the work again unless there are meaningful changes in the project approach. The new approach must clearly reflect what was learned from the previous failure and offer a better way to achieve the project objectives. (See Exhibit 8.2.)

TACTICAL PRINCIPLES FOR RUNNING PROJECTS

I have found a short list of six principles that the system builder should use when working with project teams and applying the core techniques. Use these principles when combining the core techniques to create tactics for building computer systems. These principles help you define tactics that will provide consistently good results.

1. *Every project needs a full-time leader with overall responsibility and the appropriate authority (the system builder).* There must be a single person who is responsible for the project's success and totally focused on getting the job done. This person must also have the authority to make decisions and act. It is good to have a steering committee or management oversight group in place that the system builder reports to, but a committee cannot make decisions in a timely manner. If there is no one person in this role, then the project progress and cost will reflect that—progress will be slow or nonexistent and costs will be high.

2. *Define a set of measurable and nonoverlapping objectives that are necessary and sufficient to accomplish the project goal or mission.* It is crucial that you define clear project objectives so that the people who are assigned the responsibility to achieve these objectives know what is expected of them. It is very important that the boundaries of these objectives do not overlap because, if they do, the overlap will cause confusion and conflict between the teams assigned to achieve these overlapping objectives.

   Make sure that each objective is absolutely necessary to the accomplishment of the project goal. Do not pursue an objective just because it seems like a good idea. Finally, you must be able to say that if each objective is achieved then the mission or goal has been accomplished. The objectives must cover everything that needs to happen.

3. *Assign project objectives to teams of two to seven people with hands-on team leaders and the appropriate mix of business and technical skills.* Put together a project team of two to seven people who in your judgement have among them the necessary business and technical skills and experience to address the issues that will arise in achieving the objectives you delegate to them. A team is a group of people with complementary skills who organize themselves so that all members can contribute their strengths and not be penalized for their weaknesses. Each member of the team concentrates on the aspects of designing and building the system that they are good at and/or most interested in.

For the most part, no one is required to do things they are not interested in or not good at. Within a team, the operative word is *we*, not *me*. The whole team is rewarded for successes and takes responsibility for mistakes. Singling out superstars or scapegoats undermines team morale and performance.

4. *Tell the teams WHAT to do but not HOW to do it.* Point a project team in the right direction by giving them a well-defined project goal and clearly identify the project objectives for which they are responsible. The objectives define the things that they must do to be successful. The project goal and the objectives that are delegated to a team define the game that you want that team to play. The team itself must then go through the process of creating their plan to achieve the objectives that you have laid out for them.

    General George Patton said, "Tell people what you want but don't tell them how to do it—you will be surprised by their resourcefulness in accomplishing their tasks." The teams can make changes or additions to the objectives they are given as long as you and they agree that the modified objectives are still necessary and sufficient to accomplish the project goal.

5. *Break project work into tasks that are each a week or less in duration and produce something of value to the business every 30 to 90 days.* Encourage project teams to structure their project plans so that individual tasks tend to be a week or less in duration and each task has a well defined deliverable. Track these tasks as either started, delayed, or finished. Do not fall into the trap of tracking tasks by their percentage of completion as it is unclear what "percentage complete" really means. What matters is whether the task deliverable has been produced and if not, when it will be produced.

    The system builder must be able to track progress at the task level of detail in order to understand what is really going on and to keep accurate projections of the time to complete and the cost to complete for each of the project's objectives. Multiweek tasks make progress hard to measure and they are the ones that will suddenly surprise the system builder. Multiweek tasks being reported by the percentage-complete method usually seem to be making good progress, and then in the last week they suddenly turn out to be nowhere near completion and need several more weeks to complete.

These tasks should combine to produce something that is of value to the business every 30 to 90 days. This provides the opportunity for the business to verify that the project is on the right track. It also provides deliverables that the business can start to use even before the entire project is complete to begin recouping the cost of the project.

6. *Every project needs project office staff to work with the system builder and team leaders to update plans and budgets.* The project plan and budget are analogous to the balance sheet and income statements for a business. They must be updated continuously and accurately in order to provide the people running the project with the information they need to make good decisions. There is a common but misguided notion that the system builder and team leaders should be the ones who keep the plans and budgets updated. This is analogous to the idea that the president and managers of a company should spend their time keeping the company's books.

Just as there is an accounting department to keep the company's books, there must also be a project office group that keeps project plans and budgets current. The project office staff reports to the system builder and they work with the team leaders on a weekly basis to review and update their plans and budgets. In this way the system builder can accurately monitor project progress and the team leaders are able to focus on running their teams and not filling out reports. (See Exhibit 8.3.)

EXHIBIT 8.3   TACTICAL PRINCIPLES FOR RUNNING PROJECTS

1. Every project needs a full-time leader with overall responsibility and authority.

2. Define a set of measurable and nonoverlapping objectives that are necessary and sufficient to accomplish the project goal or mission.

3. Assign project objectives to teams of 2 to 7 people with hands-on team leaders and the appropriate mix of business and technical skills.

4. Tell the teams WHAT to do but not HOW to do it.

5. Break project work into tasks that are each a week or less in duration and produce something of value to the business every 30 to 90 days.

6. Provide project office staff to work with the project leader and team leaders to update plans and budgets.

THE DEFINE–DESIGN–BUILD PROCESS

The DDB process provides a framework to guide the system builder in the selection and use of a combination of core techniques that are appropriate to any specific situation. DDB is a set of tactics or "ways to get things done" based on using different combinations of the six core techniques.

The power of DDB is that it is based on the use of this small yet comprehensive set of techniques. It is possible for everyone on a system development team to understand and use them effectively. The result is that systems get built in a very timely and efficient manner. Using the strategic guidelines and the tactical principles, the system builder can combine the six core techniques in an almost endless number of ways to meet the demands of each specific situation.

In the define phase, the system builder works with the business executives who sponsor the project. They define the business goal and the performance criteria they want to achieve. The system builder uses the strategic guidelines to create a conceptual design for a system that will achieve the criteria laid out by the business executives. The conceptual design literally is the strategy being used to accomplish the business goal. The project's objectives are then to build the various system components laid out in the conceptual design.

A cost-benefit analysis is done to evaluate whether the cost of building this system is justified by the benefits it will provide. If the costs are too high, then a different conceptual design is created that still meets most of the performance criteria and is less expensive. If a conceptual design can be created where the costs are justified by the benefits, then the initial project plan is put in place and the project moves into the design phase.

In the design phase, the system builder directs the activities of a design group that creates the detailed system design. In this phase, they build a detailed prototype of the system's user interface. People who will have to use the system get to test drive it. The group also builds a technical prototype composed of the hardware, software, and operating system specified by the system design. This verifies whether the technical components of the proposed system will work together as claimed and whether they will meet the performance levels desired.

The system design can be adjusted as needed to produce a system that will perform effectively. Changes in the user interface and the technical components of the system can be made based on test results. When the detailed design is complete, an updated project plan and budget can be put in place to guide the work in the build phase. Also, there is the option to cancel the project without a huge loss of money if the design phase shows that the system cannot be built to perform as expected at a reasonable cost.

In the build phase, the full complement of people is brought into the project and the various teams on the project focus on building the system components assigned to them—their project objectives. There should be no further design questions to answer, and everyone from the system builder to the team leaders and the individual team members can turn their full attention and energy to the job of getting the system built.

DDB is a process that uses time boxing to provide maximum traction and propel the project along. As the saying goes, "The job will expand to fill the time available." Therefore, we respond to that tendency by timeboxing our activities. When someone asks how we know that the define phase will take only two to six weeks, we answer that it will take that long because that is how much time we have allocated. That time should be sufficient for the situation confronting us. We will use selected core techniques to do a competent job, and at the end of that time we will know what we know. In light of what we know, we will either proceed into the design phase or cancel the project.

If you adhere to the time-boxing guidelines, you will quickly generate forward momentum on the project. The challenge for the project team becomes to use the relevant core techniques competently within the time allocated to get various tasks done. The challenge for the system builder is to allocate time and resources effectively. The system builder must exercise the skills of designing systems and leading projects to ensure that the project stays on track. These are demanding challenges for everyone involved and it is exhilarating to participate on a project where people rise to these challenges. (See Exhibit 8.4.)

BENEFITS OF THE DEFINE–DESIGN–BUILD PROCESS

From the perspective of the senior business executives who sponsor a system development project, the DDB process is a way to manage project risk. In the define phase, small amounts of time and money are spent up front to

EXHIBIT 8.4   THE DEFINE–DESIGN–BUILD PROCESS

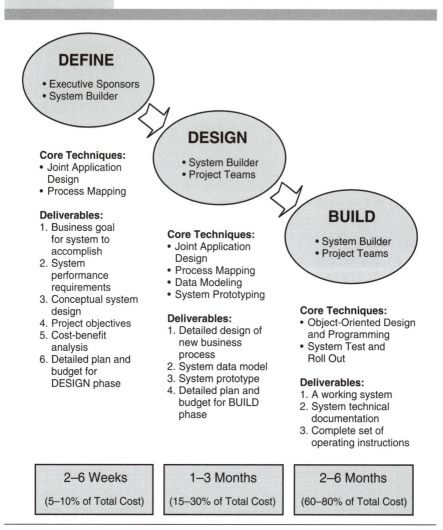

qualify a business opportunity—5 to 10% of the total project cost. If findings warrant, the company then spends only a moderate amount of further time and money in design—15 to 30% of the total project cost. In design, a small prototype system is created to prove that the opportunity is real and justifies a larger investment. The build phase is where the bulk of the time and money is spent—60 to 80% of the project total. The decision to move into build is made with the greatest amount of information. The nature of the business opportunity and the solution system that will exploit that opportunity are well established so the risk is low.

From the perspective of the system builder, the DDB process is a way to navigate through the complexity of creating a new computer system. The system builder is truly the person on the hot seat who needs to get things done. The DDB process provides a set of strategic guidelines and a tactical framework to structure the work sequence. It lets the system builder set reasonable time limits within which to investigate situations and make decisions in the define and design phases. When decisions about system design and budget have been made, this same framework provides a set of tactics for the system builder and the team leaders to employ during the build phase. The core techniques employed in the build phase give a lot of structure to the work and enable the system builder to effectively lead the effort.

From the perspective of the people on the project team, DDB is a clearly defined and manageable repertoire of techniques to work with. People who participate in the project in each of the three phases know which of the core techniques they will be expected to use in the conduct of their work. They can focus on mastering these techniques. And there is also an emphasis on working together on tasks in small groups so that the learning and use of techniques among team members is more effective than if they worked alone.

MANAGING THE ENCOUNTER WITH COMPLEXITY

DDB is a three-step sequence that could also be described as "Move it! Move it! Move it!" In order to support an agile corporation in a real-time world, systems must be built in a quick and iterative process. The time boxes for each step in this sequence are to be strictly adhered to. A disciplined and fast-paced approach is the best way to handle complexity. Complexity is as much perception as it is reality. If you allow yourself or your project teams too much time to contemplate the situations facing them they will tend to perceive excessive amounts of complexity and sink into that dreaded state called *analysis paralysis*.

Business advantage belongs to those who learn to deal well with complexity. Business initiative goes to those who learn a process that guides them in defining business opportunities and then exploiting those opportunities in a fluid and coordinated manner. One opportunity often leads to the next. Respond to each opportunity with teams of people trained to use the DDB process, and success will be yours. Define opportunities, design systems to exploit those opportunities, and quickly build those systems. As success with one opportunity opens up other opportunities, continue to respond using the DDB process. Your organization will build great competitive momentum in this way.

EXECUTIVE INSIGHT

USING INFORMATION TECHNOLOGY TO GROW THE BUSINESS

Mike Altendorf is vice president of information technology and an officer of Ace Hardware Corporation. Ace Hardware is a $3 billion company, at wholesale, that has been growing steadily in a very competitive market. There are Ace Hardware stores across North America, Central America, and South America, as well as Europe, the Middle East, and the Pacific Rim.

Mike came to his position from a career in the business side of the company, not the technical side. This makes him particularly aware of Ace business operations and the kinds of support that the company needs. His job is to identify areas of the business that can benefit from better systems support and then deliver that support. He works closely with officers and management from the different functional areas to select the most advantageous IT development projects each year.

"You can either automate what you do or you can do new things," said Mike. "That's a simple way to start evaluating the opportunities we have for new systems. We often look for opportunities where we can do something new. A good example of this the Ace Data Warehouse (ADW). We built the data warehouse over the last several years and it allows us to track sales trends and adjust prices and product offerings very quickly. This is a great tool to help us find new opportunities."

Mike described how the IT organization works with the company. "We break up into teams that focus on functional areas of the business. Leaders of these IT teams get to know their counterparts in their areas of the business and they each keep a list of possible projects." Then, starting around June each year, Mike and a subcommittee of business and technical managers convene to start the review and project selection process. "Our auditing department helps with an ROI [return on investment] calculation on the list of possible projects. We also have the functional departments rank order the projects in their areas. The third thing we do is a strategy alignment ranking. Our strategy focuses on three things—retail sales and profitability, managing the customer relationship or delivering on our "helpful" promise, and wholesale efficiency. We give each potential project a ranking for how closely it aligns with these three things."

This subcommittee narrows down the project list to a group of projects that have the most positive impact on the business and then match them with IT resources that will be available in the coming year. Then they present the list of selected projects to the full group of 13 officers (including the CEO) who run the company. This group can make any final changes that they deem necessary. Each year there are usually around 150 separate projects of different sizes scheduled for development.

Mike talked about the things he concentrates on to ensure that these projects get done in an efficient manner. The first thing is to find the right project leaders. "We are always looking for IT people who are rising leaders. We even have two career paths in IT. One path is for people who want to develop a technical focus and not have to manage people. The other path is for people who do want to manage people and projects. It's very important for project leaders to be people persons."

Mike has come to appreciate the importance of having a project management office (PMO). "We are putting a PMO into place this year. We already track project status at a high level. There is a place on our web site where people can go to see the progress on any scheduled project. Every project is in one of five phases—planned but not started, in design, in development, in beta test, or in production." The project management office will work with each project team to implement best practices, provide training on project management and to keep more detailed project plans and budgets up to date every week. People will be able to see even more clearly and quickly what is going on with each project.

Another very powerful technique has been to tie incentive bonuses to successful project completion. About 20% of the total compensation of project team members is based on these bonuses. "My director of development gets a lot of the credit for setting up this program. Project success is measured by things such as whether the project is completed on time and on budget and also on post-implementation interviews with the business users to gauge their level of satisfaction. We get over a 90% success rate now where prior to this program we were no more successful than the IT industry average—about 40 to 50%."

Endnotes

1. Sir Basil Henry Liddell Hart (1895-1970), *Strategy* (New York: Penguin Books, 1967). I came across Mr. Hart's book years ago and found Chapter 20, "The Concentrated Essence of Strategy," to have insights that are extremely relevant to the building of computer systems.
2. Kevin Kelly, *Out of Control: The Rise of Neo-Biological Civilization* (Reading, MA: Addison-Wesley, 1994). This book has many useful insights for the design and building of systems and many of these insights are summarized in Chapter 24, "The Nine Laws of God."

CHAPTER 9

A Powerful Reinforcing Feedback Loop

Now let us go into a bit more detail and see how the core techniques are combined and used in each step of the define–design–build (DDB) process to successfully build information systems. In information technology (IT) parlance this is called a *system development methodology*. DDB is a way for the system builder to think about, organize, plan, and carry out the work that needs to get done to create a new system. It is also a way for the business executive who sponsors a system development project to understand and evaluate the activities that happen as the project progresses.

DEFINE—THE FRAMEWORK FOR ACTION

It is amazing how often the define phase is overlooked or is done badly in the rush to get the project started. Yet this phase will forever either guide or confuse the project team. If done well, the clarity it provides will greatly increase the chances of the project's succeeding. If done badly, confusion will result, and the project will have very little chance of success.

The purpose of the activities in the define phase is to align the system development project with the business strategy. In this phase, the business executive who is sponsoring the system development project clearly spells out the goal or mission of the project and works with the system builder to identify the performance criteria that the system must meet.

Defining the Project Goal

The project goal should be not a technical goal. It should be a business goal—something that provides a significant business benefit or a set of benefits. It should be stated in a format that identifies an action to be taken and states the expected benefit from that action. Some examples are:

- Grow national account sales by acquiring new customers in adjacent market segments.

- Reduce complexity of steps involved in the warehouse receiving process so as to make product available for sale immediately after delivery.

The goal answers the question, "Why should we do this project?" It is a qualitative as opposed to a quantitative statement. Everyone affected by a project can quickly understand a good goal statement. A goal statement should not be longer than a sentence or two. Do not confuse a goal with a vision statement. A vision statement is a much broader statement about the organization's purpose and aspirations. A goal is one of the things an organization must accomplish in order to bring its vision to life.

Creating the Strategy

Once a goal is defined, the next step is to create a strategy to accomplish it. A strategy uses the capabilities or strengths available to a business in order to accomplish the goal. Often, a business carries out a strategy by building systems to help it do the things called for in the strategy. The sponsoring executive works with the system builder and other appropriate staff to define the strategy and the high-level or conceptual system design that supports this strategy.

To define a strategy, begin by listing a set of desired performance criteria that a system should meet in order to accomplish the goal. Robert Kaplan and David Norton, in their famous *Harvard Business Review* article "The Balanced Scorecard—Measures That Drive Performance,"[1] defined four perspectives that create a comprehensive view of an organization's performance. Describe the system's desired performance criteria from these four perspectives:

1. *Financial perspective.* What financial measures do we want the system to achieve?

2. *Customer perspective.* What do external and internal customers want from the system?

3. *Business perspective.* What business processes must we excel at to accomplish the goal?

4. *Learning perspective.* How do we continue to learn and improve our ability to accomplish this goal?

Brainstorm a list of criteria under each of the four perspectives. Then review the lists and select three to six of the most important performance criteria. If the project can build a system that meets these criteria, it shall be deemed a success.

Next, see if you can achieve these criteria in dramatically new ways. Ask the question, "What is impossible to do but, if it could be done, would dramatically change the way we do business?" Look for ways to use systems to change the business landscape, to give your organization a significant competitive advantage by doing something new and different.

The Conceptual System Design

The conceptual design is the literal embodiment of the company's strategy. The conceptual design builds upon systems and procedures that are already in place whenever possible. The conceptual design is the high-level outline of a system. Generate several different conceptual designs for systems that will meet the specified performance criteria. Express the design first as a workflow diagram or a process map.

Further define the activities in the process map by specifying the data that goes into and out of each activity. For each activity, estimate the volume and frequency of the data flows and also the source and destination of each data flow. In addition, for each activity, define the types of people (if any) who will perform this work. How many people will there be? What are the skill levels of the different types of people? Exhibit 9.1 shows the system process map for a proposed e-business system.

Next, decide which activities will be automated, which will be manual, and which will be part automated and part manual. As a rule, people like systems that automate the rote and repetitive tasks and empower them to do problem-solving and decision-making tasks more effectively. People are the spark that animates the system, and technology's role is to support that spark.

EXHIBIT 9.1   PROCESS MAP FOR E-BUSINESS SYSTEM

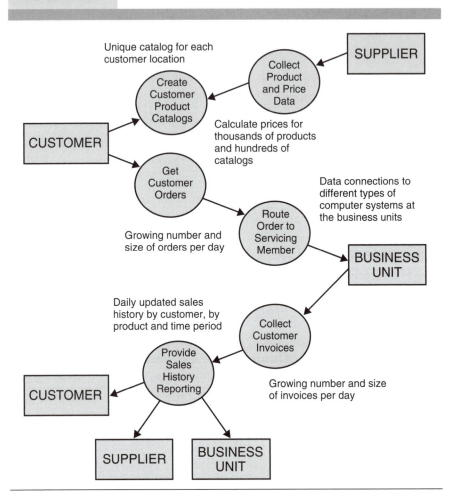

Evaluate the computer system infrastructure that already exists in the organization. Look for ways to build on it. The most cost-effective systems are those that reuse existing systems and deliver valuable new capabilities to an organization with a minimum of expense.

To get started, select the simplest combinations of technology and business processes that will meet the specified performance criteria. Balance the need for simplicity with the need to increase the capacity of the system to handle greater volumes of data and the ability to add new functionality as the business grows. Refine and improve the system as you get feedback and ideas from others.

Apply the Seven Strategic Guidelines

Conceptual system designs should respect all of the seven strategic guidelines. Under some circumstances there may be reasons to violate one or at most two of these guidelines. The only guideline that can never be violated is the first one—closely align systems development projects with business goals.

If the system devised to accomplish the business goal is in violation of one or two of the guidelines, both the executive sponsor and the system builder need to acknowledge these violations and provide justification. If only one guideline is ignored, that is acceptable. If two are ignored, there must be very good reasons for doing so. If more than two guidelines are ignored, the conceptual design is fatally flawed and should be reworked.

Define Project Objectives

When you look at the new workflows and the information system designed to support those processes, the system will resolve into a set of high-level components. Each component will be devoted to the performance of a related set of tasks, such as storing and retrieving data, helping customers find a product and place an order, or shipping products to customers.

The building of these high-level components becomes the set of objectives that is necessary and sufficient to create the system you have designed. There will tend to be somewhere between three and nine high-level components or objectives, and all other components will resolve into subcomponents of these high-level components. Strive for three to nine high-level components and not more. This is because most of us cannot comprehend at a glance or remember more than seven (plus or minus two) things at a time, and clarity of system definition and the related objectives is critical to the success of the project.

If the define phase produces a system definition that is either so broad or so complex that only a genius can understand it, then the definition is useless. Project team members will not be able to use it effectively to guide their work in the next two phases—design and build. Without a clear system definition, people on the project team will have different understandings about what the project is trying to accomplish. The people working on the different objectives will find it increasingly difficult to coordinate their actions. The level of tension and arguing will rise as the project continues.

Each of the objectives selected should be achievable in nine months or less. Each objective should provide value in its own right. An objective should not be just an intermediate step along the way that depends on the completion of some future step to be of value. Look for objectives that can be achieved quickly. These will begin providing value and repaying the cost of the project before it is even finished. Once achieved, an objective will become a base from which other objectives can be achieved.

Be careful not to define objectives that lock the project into a rigid sequence of development activities. The real world rarely goes according to plan, so the plan must be flexible in order to adapt as reality unfolds. Begin work on as many objectives as possible at the same time (work on objectives in parallel). Make the tasks needed to achieve one objective independent of the tasks needed to achieve other objectives. This provides maximum flexibility, so that if one objective is delayed, it will not also delay the completion of other objectives being done in parallel. And the system builder can shift resources from one objective to another, as needed.

The system conceptual design shown in Exhibit 9.2 has four high-level components (they are numbered on the diagram). Each of these components can provide value in its own right, and work on each component can proceed independently of the others. These four components become the four objectives for the system development project to create the system shown in this conceptual design.

Create Initial Plan and Budget

Once the three to nine objectives have been defined, a high-level project plan can be created. Create a section of the overall plan for each objective. In the section of the plan devoted to each objective, list the major tasks necessary to achieve that objective. There will be tasks related to designing and then building the deliverables necessary for each objective. Show the dependencies between the tasks and between the objectives. The plan will now reflect the strategy being used to build the systems needed to accomplish the business goal. The plan will also define the time boxes you will adhere to in the design and building of these systems.

EXHIBIT 9.2   E-BUSINESS SYSTEMS INFRASTRUCTURE:
"A WEB-ENABLED SUPPLY CHAIN"

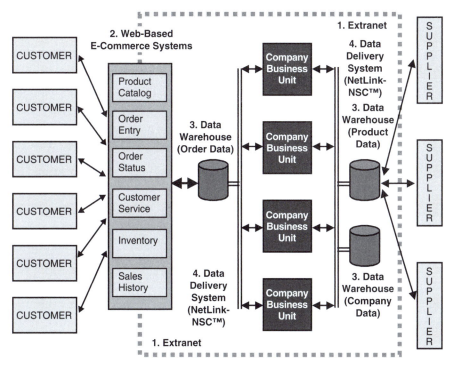

This conceptual design defines four objectives (they are numbered). Each objective can provide value in its own right. They can also be built simultaneously and independently of each other.

The greatest business value lay in the construction of the data warehouse to house the supply chain data and in building the data delivery system called NetLink-NSC™. Those components working together would best meet the supply chain performance criteria defined by the company. In order to meet financial performance criteria and reduce project risk, it was decided to lease the use of an existing Web-based product catalog and order entry system instead of building one from scratch.

In building the NetLink-NSC™ system people reused parts of an earlier system that provided for electronic receipt and error checking of customer invoices from the business units.

Source: © 2000, 2001, 2002, 2003, Network Services Company.

Estimate the total project budget by calculating the time and cost needed to achieve each project objective. Each task that is part of the plan for an objective will require some number of people with certain skills for some period of time. Multiply the standard rate for the people with these skills by the amount of time they are needed for each task. Each task will also require certain technology and perhaps other expenses, such as travel, hotel rooms, and meals. Create a spreadsheet to show these costs by task for each objective.

Once the total project cost has been estimated, do a cost-benefit analysis. If it is hard to quantify the different kinds of benefits provided by the system, this is a warning that perhaps the goal of the system is not well defined or not very valuable. If the costs of the system outweigh the benefits, find a cheaper and simpler way to accomplish the goal. Avoid the use of expensive technology that does more than is really necessary to get the job done.

Output of the Define Phase

The define phase is where the sponsoring business executives and the system builder work together to identify a business goal and a high-level system design that will accomplish that goal. This phase produces the following five deliverables:

1. *A clear statement of the business goal to be accomplished*
2. *The performance criteria required from the system.* These criteria fall into four measurement categories: (1) financial results, (2) customer expectations, (3) critical business operations, and (4) learning and ongoing improvement. These are the conditions of success that the system must meet.
3. *Strategy and conceptual design for a system to accomplish the business goal and meet the performance criteria.* The system design is composed of people, process, and technology. The conceptual design is the embodiment of the strategy being used to attain the goal.
4. *A definition of the project objectives that are needed (necessary and sufficient) to build the system.* The objectives are the things that must be built to create the system outlined in the conceptual design.
5. *A cost-benefit analysis that verifies that the project is worth carrying out.* The senior business executive who is responsible for accomplishing the business goal that the system will address must confirm that this analysis is valid. (See Exhibit 9.3.)

EXHIBIT 9.3   DEFINE PHASE

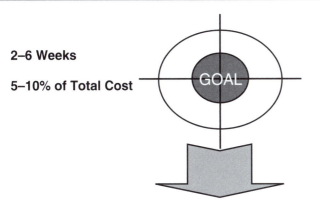

2–6 Weeks

5–10% of Total Cost

The GOAL is the target or the mission. Make it clear. In two sentences or less, state the action and the desired result. Also state the performance criteria needed to reach the goal.

1. Devise a STRATEGY to accomplish this GOAL that maximizes the use of the organization's resources and the things that it does well.

2. Express this strategy as a PROCESS flow that will meet certain performance criteria (financial, customer, operations, learning).

3. Specify how PEOPLE fit into the flow. Define the TECHNOLOGY that will support the process and the people. You now have a CONCEPTUAL SYSTEM DESIGN.

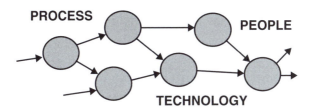

4. Identify the necessary and sufficient set of measurable achievements needed to build this system — these are the project OBJECTIVES.

Objective A (Time and Cost)	Objective B (Time and Cost)	Objective C (Time and Cost)	Objective D (Time and Cost)

5. The Initial PROJECT PLAN and BUDGET is the sum of the estimated times and costs for each project objective.

6. Use cost-benefit analysis to verify that the conceptual system design will accomplish its goal in a cost-effective manner. Modify the conceptual system design if necessary to reduce cost.

DESIGN—WORKFLOW AND SYSTEM DESIGN

The purpose of the design phase is to flesh out the conceptual design and create the detailed specifications. The phase begins with the system builder's reviewing the project goal, the conceptual system design, and the project objectives with the project work group. The work group is composed of business and technical people who have the necessary mix of business and technical skills and experience needed to do the detailed system design.

It is important for people to understand senior management's intentions and the project's goal. Specific issues relating to the project objectives and budget can be investigated during this phase. If necessary, adjustments can be made in light of the findings that come out of this phase. There are three things that need to be done in the design phase:

1. Create detailed process map diagrams for the new system.
2. Define the logical data model.
3. Build and test the system prototype (i.e., the user interface and the technical architecture).

Divvy up the time allotted to the design phase among these three activities. Give each activity the time needed to do a competent job. Avoid the temptation to spend extra time doing excessive amounts of analysis and checking and rechecking the results that come out of each activity.

It is important to keep the people who are doing the work on these three activities working together. System process maps, system data models, and system prototypes are just different aspects of the same system. The designs created for these three aspects must be created in concert with each other or else they will not fit together. The work in these three areas needs to be done simultaneously.

Use the joint application design (JAD) technique to integrate the work of people who focus on the three different aspects. As the team defines the details of the business process map, the data modelers can record the data needed by the process. As the process requirements and the types and volumes of data become clear, the technical architecture can be defined and tested to see if it will support the process and the data. As the process flow, the data model, and the technical architecture are defined, people can design the user interface needed to fit the process flow and handle the related data.

The Role of the System Builder

There is a natural tendency for a communication gap to exist between business and technical people. It is up to the system builder to create an inclusive design process that involves both kinds of people and bridges the gap between them. It is common for people to rush to conclusions about how a process should work or what kind of technology should be used. If the system builder can tolerate not knowing and sets an example of reserving judgment and taking the time allocated to work through different design options, then the creative power of the people on the project begins to open up.

The system builder needs to push the people on the project to keep looking for the simple underlying patterns that define an effective business process. The system builder needs to lead the search for elegantly simple ways to support this process with technology. The more complex the designs for a system become, the harder the system is to build and the lower the probability that the project will succeed.

The Design Process

The first part of the design phase should be spent in JAD sessions in which the business and technical people explore different process designs. Here is where people should "think outside the box" and generate as many ideas as possible. The team then needs to select the most useful ideas and fit them together to form a coherent and detailed map of how work will be organized and how things will be done in the new business process flow.

Once the process flows have been sketched out, then the JAD sessions can begin to focus on the how technology will be used to support this process. The design team starts to define how people in the process will interact with the technology supporting the process. Often, designing this user interface takes the form of creating a sequence of screens that people will use.

When designing the user interface, look for ways to automate the rote and repetitive work. People don't like to do this kind of work—it is usually boring and computers do that kind of task very well. Look for ways to empower the problem-solving and decision-making tasks. Design systems that will be a rewarding experience for people to work with.

If the decision is made to use a packaged software application, then that package should be brought in and installed in a test environment. Realistic usage scenarios should be scripted out. The databases used by the package must be loaded with a sampling of real data. People who will both use and support the package then need to evaluate it by working through the usage scenarios.

The technical people who will be responsible for building the system should sit in on the JAD sessions. As the design unfolds, they should be selecting technology—hardware, databases, and software that will effectively support the system being designed. They should participate and listen to what the businesspeople need in order to do their jobs. They should not slow down or confuse the design process with excessively technical questions or long dissertations on this or that technical subject.

During the design phase it may become clear that a given performance criterion cannot be met. It may become clear that the initial conceptual design from the define phase is not quite right and must be modified. Because of this, certain project objectives might be redefined. The project goal must remain unchanged, but specific performance criteria needed to accomplish the goal can be changed if needed. The system builder is the liaison between senior management and the project work group when it comes to this redefinition process.

Creation of the Detailed Project Plan and Budget

Toward the end of the design phase, as the detailed design specifications are produced, everyone involved should have a clear idea of the work they need to do and how long this will take in the build phase. The system builder should then let each team define how they will do their work and figure out how long it will take. The teams should be challenged to set ambitious but achievable time frames.

Teams should be encouraged to break their work into discreet tasks that take one week or less. This is because a week is the standard unit of time in business and teams must strive to accomplish something of measurable value each week. A project plan that clearly lays out for every person what he or she is expected to accomplish every week is a valuable tool for coordinating and monitoring the work of building the system. A plan at this level of detail is also the best way to arrive at an accurate and realistic project budget for the build phase.

As the project teams are each creating their specific task plans to achieve the objectives assigned to them, the system builder is combining these plans into the overall project plan. In a process that is somewhat analogous to the manner in which a general plans a campaign, the system builder plans the sequence of activities that will lead to the successful building of the system that the design phase has specified.

Divide or segment the overall project plan by objective. There is a section of the plan devoted to each objective. The system builder determines the necessary sequence for achieving project objectives and arranges the project plan to reflect this. Task plans created by the project teams for each objective are inserted into the sections of the project plan devoted to the relevant objectives.

Look for opportunities to run activities in parallel. The more work that can be done simultaneously, the more flexible the project will be. When activities are run in sequence, a delay in one activity causes a ripple effect that delays all the other activities queued up behind it. When activities are run in parallel, a delay in one does not delay the others.

Activities should create deliverables that come together and combine at the end to achieve the objective. By running in parallel, it allows the opportunity to finish one activity and then shift resources over to help out on another activity that is delayed. Delays are inevitable on a project. Any plan that does not account for delays and provide the flexibility needed to effectively respond to them is a plan whose timetable and budget will quickly be thrown into disarray.

The Decision to Proceed or Not to Proceed

If there are doubts about the viability of the project or if the revised budget has gotten too big, now is the time to reduce the scope of the project or cancel it altogether. At this point only 20 to 40% of the total project cost will have been incurred. The business has yet to commit the major effort on the project.

It is all too common for organizations to run the design phase as a poorly defined research project. Much time is spent in detailed analysis of what already exists, but only sketchy design work is done on the specifics of what the new system will be. Debates break out on many aspects of the design of the new system, but no clear answers are agreed upon.

The design phase is the opportunity for a company to reduce the risk on a project before committing large amounts of time and money to it. The more detailed the design specifications, the better the chances for building the system on time and on budget. The broader the understanding of and support for the system among both the business and the technical people, the greater the likelihood that the system will be used effectively and produce the desired business results.

Design Phase Deliverables

In the design phase the system builder and the project work group flesh out the conceptual system design. They produce the detailed design specifications necessary to guide the work of building the system and to accurately estimate the cost of building the system. They also create prototypes of the system's technical architecture and its user interface in order to verify that the system will perform as expected. There are four deliverables produced in this phase:

1. *A detailed process map for the new system workflows.* The specifications for the new system workflows are created using the process-mapping technique and captured in documents such as process diagrams and process logic descriptions for each activity or task in the process. Also there must be agreement among the people who will have to work with the new system that it will meet the performance criteria expected of it.

2. *A system data model that accommodates the data required by the business process model.* The data model should be in a form that is understandable by other people on the project. In addition, the model should record the volume of data that will be handled and the frequency with which different types of data will be accessed.

3. *A system prototype that specifies both the technical architecture and the user interface.* There should be a development environment in operation wherein all the components of the technical architecture are installed and working together. This technical architecture must be shown to be capable of handling the data volumes and user demands that are expected. The user interface needed to support the process logic in the relevant steps of the process flow should be defined. There must be a complete set of screen layouts, report formats, and specifications for all aspects of the user interface.

4. *A detailed project plan and budget that accurately reflects the time, cost and resources needed to build the system.* No plan can predict the future or anticipate all obstacles and no budget can accurately estimate every cost. However, plans and budgets that are built up from the detail task level and structured to provide as much flexibility as possible are essential to guiding the project to a successful conclusion. (See Exhibit 9.4.)

BUILD—SYSTEM CONSTRUCTION AND ROLLOUT

The build phase is where the project effort really ramps up. The full complement of people is brought into the project to fill out the project teams. Because of this, the weekly cost or "burn rate" on the project rises significantly in the build phase. Unlike the previous two phases, the cost of false starts and wrong turns now adds up very quickly. This is where the system builder gets to vigorously exercise the skills of project leadership. Activity must be tightly focused on the completion of defined tasks necessary to achieve the project objectives. This is the phase where good design and planning pay off handsomely.

The System Blueprints

The initial work in this phase is to create the system object model from the combination of specification from the data model and the system prototype. This activity is often started in the design phase as part of the detail design and budgeting process. By completing the work at the appropriate level of detail, the project teams produce very detailed blueprints of what they will build. This builds the teams' understanding of and confidence in their ability to do the work.

These system blueprints take the form of the screen layouts, the database design, the system object model, and the detailed technical architecture diagrams. These documents guide and structure the work that creates the actual system. The system builder and the team leaders track their progress every week using these documents to discuss relevant details.

The system database and software are created and tested in the system development environment. The development environment is created in the design phase to support the prototyping of the technical architecture and

EXHIBIT 9.4   DESIGN PHASE

1–3 Months

15–30% of Total Cost

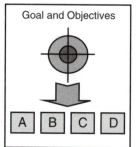

Goal and Objectives

The system builder reviews with the project work group the GOAL, the conceptual system design, and the project OBJECTIVES that were set by senior management.

Project teams use core techniques to flesh out the conceptual design and create detailed system designs and specifications.

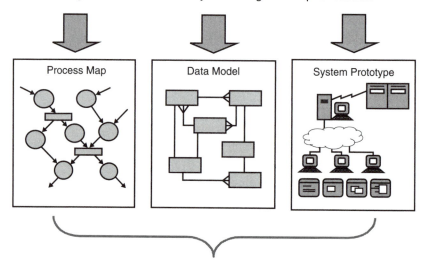

Process Map

Data Model

System Prototype

Detailed system specifications allow the creation of a detailed project plan and budget.

Project Plan and Budget		Cost
Objective A		
Task 1		
Task 2		
Task 3		$999
Objective B		
Task 4		
Task 5		$99
Objective C		
Task 6		$999
Task 7		
Total Project		$9,999

the user interface. It is composed of the actual hardware, operating systems, and database packages that will be used to build the system. Also installed in the development environment are any preprogrammed application software packages that will be used for parts or all of the system.

Once programming begins, progress gets recorded at the object level using the object chart as the reporting tool. As work is begun on an object, that object gets circled. Everyone can see how long the work should take. As the work is completed, the object gets colored in. People can tell at a glance by looking at the object model what is the progress on software development. When problems develop the system builder and team leaders using the object model can quickly see what objects are affected and what the issues are. They can then focus on specific solutions for well-defined problems.

If software development projects are not tracked at this level of detail, then people will resort to the infamous "percentage complete" method. Under this method, what happens is that large multiweek tasks quickly become "70% complete" (whatever that means). Then the last 30% takes four times as long to finish as the first 70% and nobody can figure out why.

The Project Office

It is through the assistance of the project office that the system builder is able to effectively coordinate and focus the activities on a fast-paced project. There must be skilled staff dedicated solely to working with the system builder and the team leaders to update the project plan and budget as work progresses.

The system builder is analogous to the president of a company, and the project office is like the accounting department. The president does not have time to keep the company's books nor is that the president's job. But if no one is keeping the books, the president will lose touch with where the company really stands, and this will inevitably lead to bad decisions.

There is a pervasive tendency for people to hide bad news such as delays and cost overruns. Unless the system builder takes active steps to counter this tendency, there will be trouble. People need to see that they will not be penalized for reporting bad news. On the contrary, they must be shown that by reporting delays and potential cost overruns as soon as they perceive them, they can improve their chances of success because they have more time to react.

Early reporting gives everyone more time to respond effectively. People need to understand that the project office staff is there to help them keep track of what is really going on and make good decisions. Indeed, one of the best ways to get into trouble is to hide bad news, because when the truth finally does come out, there is usually very little if any time to respond effectively to the situation.

Lead by Staying Involved

The system builder relies on a mixture of information obtained from the updated project plan and budget and from personal visits and investigations into areas of the project that attract attention. This person cannot spend undue time in his or her office reading e-mails and writing memos. The system builder holds regular weekly meetings with all project leaders to review their sections of the project plan. As problems show up, the system builder continuously assesses when to get personally involved and when to delegate to others.

Obstacles will arise and delays will happen—it is inevitable. The system builder who has built flexibility into the project plan and who has people on the project that can be shifted from one objective to another has options. Systems that use simple combinations of technology and business process to achieve multiple objectives are more likely to be built on time and on budget. With systems like this, a system builder can quickly shift resources from one objective to another because the same skill sets and technologies are being used to achieve different system objectives.

System Test and Rollout

As major system components or subsystems are delivered, they go into beta test with a pilot group of businesspeople. This pilot group should have been involved in some way in the design phase of the project. In this way, they will already have an understanding and acceptance of the need for and benefits of the new system so they will be good beta test personnel.

Adjustments will need to be made to the system architecture and to the user interface during the beta test. People who operate the system architecture will need to tweak different operating parameters to get the best response time and stability from the system. People who designed the user interface will need to sit with the pilot group of business users and listen to their ideas for improvements to certain screens.

As businesspeople in the pilot group test the system and make suggestions for adjustments, the rough edges are smoothed off. In this process, advocates for the system will emerge from among the pilot group. They will feel a personal connection to the success of the system because the system will take on a look and feel that is influenced by their suggestions. These are the people who will sell the benefits of the system to the rest of the company and who will often be the ones to train their coworkers in the use of the new system.

Build Phase Deliverables

The build phase is where most of the work and most of the cost occur. However, if the first two phases—define and design—where done well, this phase will have a manageable level of risk and it can be completed successfully. If the first two phases were not well done, this phase cannot be successful. The three deliverables from this phase are:

1. *A working system that matches the design specifications and meets the performance criteria.* The building of the system should be scheduled so that there is something of value delivered to the business every 30 to 90 days. This means that certain pieces of the system must be finished and put into use before the entire system is completed.

2. *A complete and updated set of technical design documents.* The design documentation is analogous to the wiring diagrams and structural plans of a building. This is the documentation that enables the business that owns the system to build enhancements and make repairs to the system in the future. The documentation should include at least the object model, the data model, an organized library of program source code, and diagrams and descriptions of the overall process flow of the system.

3. *A complete set of operating instructions.* The people who operate and maintain a system are different from the people who build systems. The people who operate a system need to know how bring the system up, bring it down, do performance tuning, and do troubleshooting and operating maintenance. The people who will be responsible for operating a new system need to work with the development team during system rollout to define the needed operating and maintenance documentation. (See Exhibit 9.5.)

EXHIBIT 9.5   BUILD PHASE

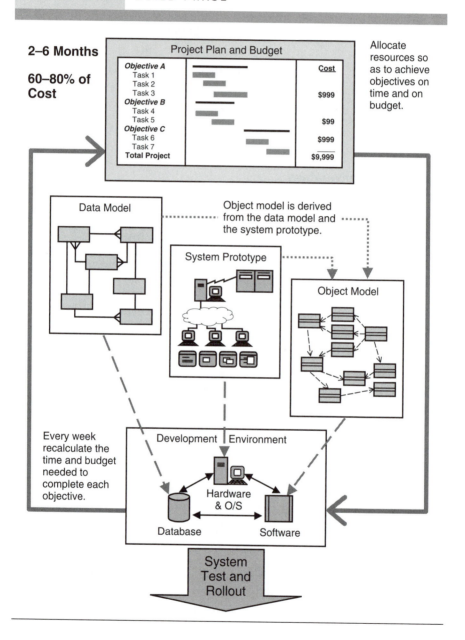

TWO WINS, A LOSE, AND A DRAW

Here, I present four real projects from my own experience as a way to examine what works and what does not. These were all prominent, multimillion-dollar system development projects. On three of them I was the overall project leader or system builder. On the other one I was one of four team leaders—there was no system builder. They span the years from the early 1990s to the early 2000s. Two of these projects were major successes, one was an utter failure, and one was not a complete failure but it was not a success either.

These projects used a range of technologies—IBM mainframes with COBOL and DB2, Sun servers running Java and Sybase, and NT servers with SQL server databases accessed through Windows PCs and Web-based thin clients. Although the technology and the business goals were different for each of these projects, I saw that there was a consistency to the reasons why projects succeed or fail.

I learned that the seven strategic system design guidelines and the six principles for running projects really work and that there are consequences if you ignore them. I also saw that the core techniques (the skills of the game) were applicable each time regardless of the technology being used. These guidelines, principles, and core techniques represent a body of knowledge that must be understood and applied in order to succeed.

Finally, I saw that there is a basic, underlying sequence to the process of building computer systems. That sequence is define–design–build. Depending on the system development methodology you are using or the consulting company you may be working with, there could officially be a much more complicated process in place. The define phase can be divided into two or more steps with important sounding names such as "Preliminary Needs Analysis" or "System Concept Justification." The design phase may be fractured into three or four steps with more fancy titles, and the build phase can be broken into a further number of steps.

However, this complexity neither increases people's chances of success nor changes the basic sequence of things that have to happen. First, one must define what is to be done. Next, one must design how it will be done. And finally, one must do it—build it.

What can be learned here? To begin with, every project needs a qualified, full-time project leader or system builder who has full responsibility and day-to-day authority for running the entire project. Working with the senior businessperson who is the executive sponsor, the system builder identifies a specific business opportunity and defines the system performance criteria needed to exploit that opportunity. Without a person in this role, confusion will reign.

Projects should be focused on developing new system capabilities not already available in existing systems. It is best to combine new technology with existing systems to create new systems. Do not try to recreate functions that already exist in older systems that are working well enough. It will be too costly and not deliver enough value if you rip out existing systems and replace them with new technology that does essentially the same things.

By building upon existing systems, a much simpler set of new technology can often be used. PC workstations can be used to run terminal emulation software to let people access existing mainframe systems. New applications can be Web or server based. The whole mix of new and old applications can be integrated under a single graphical user interface by giving each application an icon that users click on to switch from one application to another.

Employ the time boxes suggested in the define–design–build process and move the project along at a fast clip. It is very important to set and maintain a brisk pace on a project or else it tends to degenerate into a sluggish and indecisive voyage to nowhere. Use the overall time boxes suggested for each phase and then subdivide these boxes into smaller boxes for each of the major activities that are defined in a phase. Further subdivide those activity time boxes into task-level time boxes. The trick is to define time boxes that are both aggressive and realistic.

There is a very effective approach demonstrated in both of the projects that succeeded. Simply stated, this approach is a matter of first focusing the development effort to create a breakthrough deliverable. This is a deliverable that proves the system and wins over lots of supporters. Once the breakthrough is achieved, every effort should be made to exploit it quickly by developing more system enhancements and new subsystems to address further opportunities opened up by the breakthrough.

The charts shown in Exhibits 9.6 through 9.9 are maps of the four projects. They show how each one unfolded over time. Study the sequence of activities, read the notes that explain these activities, and you will gain a quick, overall appreciation of each project. Underneath every chart is a brief description of what happened.

EXHIBIT 9.6   AN ENTERPRISE SALES SUPPORT SYSTEM—
A WIN

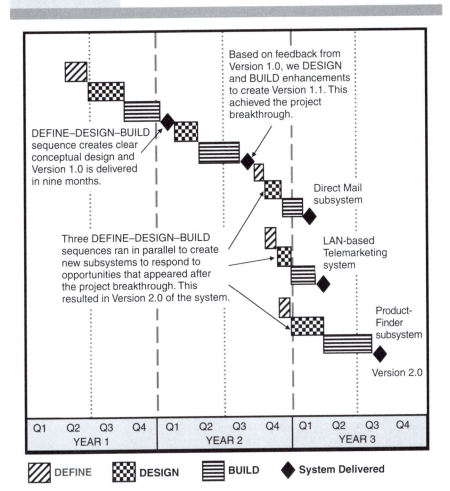

Based on feedback from Version 1.0, we DESIGN and BUILD enhancements to create Version 1.1. This achieved the project breakthrough.

DEFINE–DESIGN–BUILD sequence creates clear conceptual design and Version 1.0 is delivered in nine months.

Three DEFINE–DESIGN–BUILD sequences ran in parallel to create new subsystems to respond to opportunities that appeared after the project breakthrough. This resulted in Version 2.0 of the system.

Direct Mail subsystem

LAN-based Telemarketing system

Product-Finder subsystem

Version 2.0

Q1	Q2	Q3	Q4	Q1	Q2	Q3	Q4	Q1	Q2	Q3	Q4
	YEAR 1				YEAR 2				YEAR 3		

▨ DEFINE   ▦ DESIGN   ☰ BUILD   ◆ System Delivered

This development sequence narrowed scope and focused resources up front to create version one of the system and achieve the project breakthrough point. Once the breakthrough had been achieved, multiple DEFINE–DESIGN–BUILD sequences were launched in parallel to exploit the opportunities that opened up.

I followed all the strategic design guidelines. The tactical principles for running projects were followed although there was no staff devoted exclusively to the project office function. The team leaders and I did the project office work and at times we did not keep plans and budgets up to date. If the project had been any larger, the lack of dedicated project office staff would have hurt us.

EXHIBIT 9.7   A WEB-ENABLED SUPPLY CHAIN—A WIN

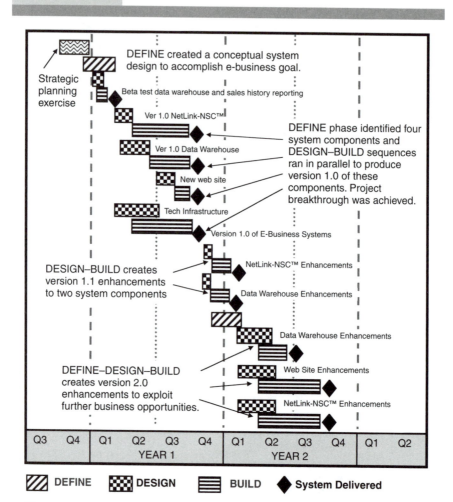

The development sequence was focused and tightly time-boxed. Work ran in parallel during the DESIGN-BUILD phases requiring good planning and coordination. Version 1.0 of the e-business systems infrastructure was created in nine months. Based on positive reception and feedback from version 1.0, enhancements for version 1.1 were created. Further assessment of business needs led to definition of next round of major enhancements that created version 2.0 of the e-business infrastructure.

I followed all of the seven strategic design guidelines and respected the six tactical principles for running projects. This project was a clear demonstration of how to quickly and cost-effectively design and build a suite of new systems that provide a significant competitive advantage.

EXHIBIT 9.8   THE NEW TECHNOLOGY FOR SALES
PROJECT—A LOSE

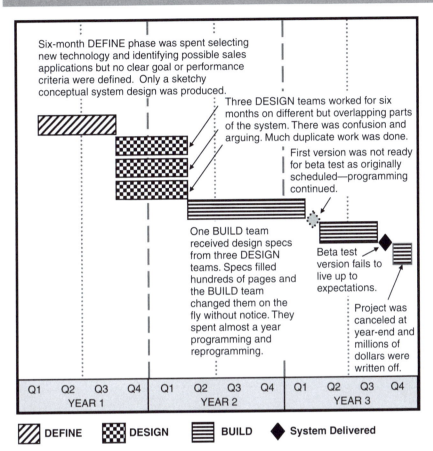

Six-month DEFINE phase was spent selecting new technology and identifying possible sales applications but no clear goal or performance criteria were defined. Only a sketchy conceptual system design was produced.

Three DESIGN teams worked for six months on different but overlapping parts of the system. There was confusion and arguing. Much duplicate work was done.

First version was not ready for beta test as originally scheduled—programming continued.

One BUILD team received design specs from three DESIGN teams. Specs filled hundreds of pages and the BUILD team changed them on the fly without notice. They spent almost a year programming and reprogramming.

Beta test version fails to live up to expectations.

Project was canceled at year-end and millions of dollars were written off.

Q1	Q2	Q3	Q4	Q1	Q2	Q3	Q4	Q1	Q2	Q3	Q4
	YEAR 1				YEAR 2				YEAR 3		

DEFINE   DESIGN   BUILD   ◆ System Delivered

On this project there was a long DEFINE phase that resulted in a broad project scope. There was no clear focus of effort. Resources were then spread across several different DESIGN teams who developed complex designs. Design specifications were handed off to a BUILD team that was overwhelmed by the amount of work required. Momentum was lost and a breakdown occurred in the BUILD phase. Programmers worked long and hard but the project never recovered.

I was one of four team leaders. There was no overall project manager or system builder to answer questions or resolve disputes. The strategic design guidelines were completely ignored — some deliberately and some out of carelessness. Most of the tactical principles for running projects were violated. Project teams did have two to seven people and we did have freedom to figure out how to do our work, but we still did not know exactly what we were supposed to do. So there was much arguing and everything took forever.

EXHIBIT 9.9   NEXT GENERATION FINANCIAL SERVICES
                SYSTEM—A DRAW

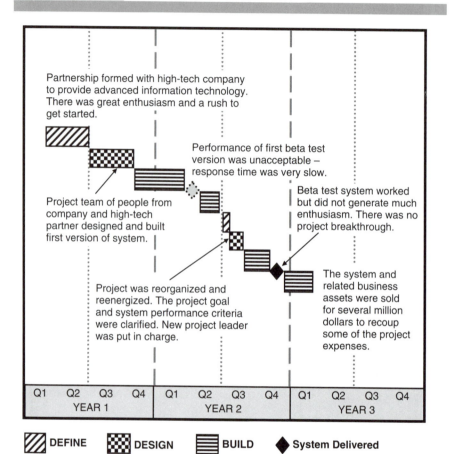

Partnership formed with high-tech company to provide advanced information technology. There was great enthusiasm and a rush to get started.

Performance of first beta test version was unacceptable – response time was very slow.

Project team of people from company and high-tech partner designed and built first version of system.

Beta test system worked but did not generate much enthusiasm. There was no project breakthrough.

Project was reorganized and reenergized. The project goal and system performance criteria were clarified. New project leader was put in charge.

The system and related business assets were sold for several million dollars to recoup some of the project expenses.

| Q1 | Q2 | Q3 | Q4 | Q1 | Q2 | Q3 | Q4 | Q1 | Q2 | Q3 | Q4 |
| YEAR 1 | | | | YEAR 2 | | | | YEAR 3 | | | |

▨ DEFINE   ▨ DESIGN   ▤ BUILD   ◆ System Delivered

The project got off to an adequate start, but then faltered because the technology did not perform up to expectations and the business logic was not accurately captured during the DESIGN phase. The project was reorganized and reenergized but no fundamental changes were made in technology or project scope. The renewed effort produced some better results but not enough to gain acceptance of the system from target customers.

I was the new project leader brought in when the project was reorganized. I followed all the tactical principles for running projects and applied them vigorously. The project was closely aligned with a business goal and there was some flexibility in both the project plan and the project staff. However, the other five strategic guidelines were not followed. I learned what many have learned before—great tactics cannot make up for flawed strategy.

ENDNOTE

1. Robert Kaplan and David Norton, "The Balanced Scorecard—Measures That Drive Performance," *Harvard Business Review* (January–February 1992), pg. 71–79.

CHAPTER 10

The Illusion of Control

As business becomes more engaged in the real-time world, the traditional concepts and practices of control are changing. The time-honored notions of command and control in the hierarchically structured company are giving way to new ideas about coordination and organization. This chapter looks at what happens to us and to our companies when we start using new ways of motivating people and new ways of organizing work. It offers some insights into what lies ahead for businesses and our economy.

> *Success in business depends less on rote and more on reason;*
> *less on the authority of the few and more on the judgement of the many;*
> *less on compulsion and more on motivation;*
> *less on external control of people and more on internal discipline.*
>
> —Dee Hock, founder and CEO emeritus of Visa International[1]

FLOCKS AND SWARMS

What makes a flock of birds or a school of hundreds of fish move as if they are a single entity? What makes them all suddenly turn at the same time? There is something more subtle at work here than just a leader bird or a captain fish telling all the others what to do. What can we learn from these dynamics that is relevant to the way we structure and operate a real-time business?

There seems to be some kind of instantaneous and all-pervasive communication at work when we observe the sudden twists and turns of a flock of birds or a school of fish. We call this "swarming behavior." Whatever the mode of communication that may be at work with birds and fish, many of us now own an item that is capable of producing swarming behavior in us. That item is the mobile phone.[2] And that item is evolving before our very eyes because so many people are using it for so many different but related forms of communication. In its latest incarnation, the item is a combination phone, digital camera, Web browser, and instant messaging device.

Think like a kid and write down a list of at least 20 cool things you could do in your organization if everybody in it had a current-generation mobile phone. In other words, think about how the business could operate differently and more profitably if everyone had instantaneous voice, data, and video communication as well as Web access and e-mail. If you choose not to do this, at least admit that your competition is doing it and at some point they are going to come up with something very powerful that will catch you way off guard.

For starters, consider this. It is easy to combine global positioning system data (GPS data) with data from mobile phones. An organization whose members all have current-generation mobile phones can now create a single big picture view or map of their world that is created from the eyes of all the people in the organization. This view can be updated in real time to reflect changes in that world. People can access relevant parts of the big picture to get the information they need to make their next move. As long as people all have a common understanding of what they are trying to accomplish, everyone will act with a common purpose without needing to be told what to do. This is swarming behavior. It is fast, powerful, and continuously responding to change.

THE DECENTRALIZATION OF INFORMATION AND CONTROL

The very existence of the agile real-time organization is based on everyone in the organization having the same big-picture view of his or her world. Everyone does not need access to all the detail, but everyone does need access to meaningful summaries and indicators of business activity and performance in each area of the company. And this information needs to be kept current, hour by hour and day to day.

When everyone knows what their objectives or performance targets are and when they can see moment to moment what is going on and whether those operations are on target or off target, then something powerful starts to happen.[3] Swarming behavior emerges as people learn how their individual behaviors combine to create larger effects. Those larger effects are organizational responses that move their organization toward achieving its performance targets even as the world continues to change.

No one person can do it alone, but swarms of people can cause an organization to become alive. They can bring about organizational behavior that yields continuous efficiency and profitability from a thousand small wins as well as a few big wins. When customer service people start working more effectively with salespeople, when salespeople start working more effectively with credit and accounting people, when those people start working more effectively with marketing people, and information technology (IT) people start working more effectively with everybody—well, then amazing things happen.

Decentralization of information is accomplished by giving everyone in the organization a common big-picture view of the total organization. Each person also gets access to the relevant detail information to support the particular activities he or she is responsible for. This allows people to see how their individual performance relates to the performance of the whole company.

Decentralization of control is accomplished by giving everyone a clear set of performance targets that they are supposed to achieve. Performance targets define the results that are expected, but people figure out for themselves how to deliver those results. The speed and efficiency demanded of real-time organizations can occur only if people think for themselves and control their own actions.

However, it is very important to note that decentralization of control is not democracy. The executives in charge of a company still set the organization's strategy and performance targets. They also set the operating parameters that each business unit needs to abide by. Business units are not at liberty to change company strategy or performance targets or to stray outside of their operating parameters. Only within the boundaries set by operating parameters and performance targets are individual business units free to decide and act on their own initiative.

THE GREAT GAME OF BUSINESS

The real-time enterprise requires the full participation of all the people in the organization. They need to be attuned to the daily operations in a way that is not required in a traditional Industrial Age company. People need to be focused on the status of the company and their own specific operations and know how what they do will influence the status of the whole company. This is the context that provides everyone with the opportunity to make effective decisions on their own in real time and, at the same time, work for the overall good of the organization.

How can people be motivated to transform the way they participate in that activity we all call "work"? Business has been using the team metaphor for some time now, yet it is rare to see the kind of real teamwork and team spirit in business that we all respond to when we watch a winning sports team rise to the challenge and clinch a championship title. The good news is that the answer is staring us right in the face. We are social creatures—we love to play games, and business is a game.

It is through playing games that we all began to learn when we were children. It is through games that we will learn what we need to know to thrive in the real-time world. The game analogy to business is actually much more accurate than the war or battle analogy. The use of the word *game* in no way trivializes or minimizes the seriousness of the undertaking. Ask any professional golfer or basketball player or soccer player, they know full well how serious a game is.

When people have a personal stake in the outcome of a game, they become interested in that game. When people are interested in something, they pay attention and learn quickly. I am always amazed when people who at first appear to be not very well educated or to not know very much can suddenly tell me volumes when a subject arises that interests them. People can reel off names and statistics about their favorite teams, they can guide me through the intricacies of reading a racing form that describes the horses and riders in a race, or they can tell me everything about the history and most likely future behaviors of the characters in a soap opera. People can create fantasy sports teams by combining players in a sport just as skillfully as a mutual funds manager creates a winning portfolio by combining stocks of different companies.

Senior managers and entrepreneurs already know how to play the great game of business because they all have significant reasons to be very interested and to become very knowledgeable about it. To be a successful real-time enterprise, everybody in the organization needs to have a keen interest in the organization's performance, and they must constantly be learning to improve their performance and that of the organization. Any company can acquire and install technology, so technology alone cannot constitute a significant or long-lasting competitive advantage. Sustainable advantage comes only from the skill of the players and the way they play the game.

In his book, *The Great Game of Business,*[4] Jack Stack speaks from experience and describes the techniques his company uses to support this approach to business. He is the CEO of a company called Springfield ReManufacturing Corporation. In the early 1980s it was a nearly bankrupt division of International Harvester, and Jack had been sent out to shut it down. Instead, he and a group of other managers put up their own money and took out a bank loan to buy the company. Their bank required them to provide weekly balance sheets and income statements to monitor the situation since the business was so deeply in debt.

Jack and the other managers quickly realized that they needed everybody in the company pulling in the same direction and putting their hearts into it or else the company would not make it. They taught everybody how to read balance sheets and income statements (easy compared to reading racing forms) and provided people with even more detailed income statements that related to their individual departments. Then they defined quarterly performance targets and paid out bonuses of up to 13% of base salaries if the company hit or exceeded its quarterly targets. If targets were not met, then there was no payout at all. But every quarter, the game began again so people could learn and quickly apply what they had learned in the following quarter. Over the next several years, they learned very well. The company pulled out of debt and has thrived since then.

Jack Stack defines four basic conditions needed to start and sustain the great game of business:

1. *People must understand the rules of the game and how it is played.* They must know what is fair and what is not fair and how to score points.

2. *People must be able to pick the roles or positions they want to play in the game.* They also need to get the training and experience necessary to keep developing the skills needed to succeed in their positions.

3. *All players must know what the score is at all times.* They need to know if they are winning or losing and they need to see the results of their actions.

4. *All players must have a personal stake in the outcome of the game.* There must be some important reward (usually monetary) that provides a reason for each player to strive to succeed.

HARNESSING THE POWER OF THE SELF-ADJUSTING FEEDBACK LOOP

A powerful feedback loop emerges when people's interactions with each other are cast in the form of a game whose object is to achieve specified performance targets. If people in a company have real-time access to the data they need, then they will steer toward their targets. If they are rewarded when they achieve their targets, then they will learn to hit those targets more often than not. The profit potential of the self-adjusting feedback loop is now unleashed.

Markets are constantly moving and changing. Product life cycles are measured in months or a few years, no longer in decades. Companies cannot fine-tune their operations to fit a present set of conditions and then expect to simply run those operations unchanged for years and years. That was the old industrial model. The world has changed, and that model no longer yields the profits we seek. We need something much more responsive—something that constantly adjusts to changes and opportunities.

The effect of a thousand small adjustments in a company and in the operating processes of that company as its markets change is like the effect of compound interest. At first hearing, one might not appreciate the profound result on capital accumulation over time as relatively low rates of interest are applied to an initial capital base. But the capital base grows, so the net amount of new capital generated from the same low interest rates begins to rise exponentially.

By analogy, a real-time organization that can constantly make small adjustments to better respond to its changing environment will both cut its costs and increase its revenues. No one adjustment by itself will be all that significant, but the cumulative effect over time will be enormous. And companies that cannot earn profits from constant small adjustments will hardly be profitable at all.

A Coercive System—The Dark Side

What we have described in this chapter is the response to the real-time world that will prove to be the most constructive and the one that generates the most wealth for the most people. But it is naive to think that people will not also use real-time technology to impose extreme command and control regimes on their organizations. Those who crave the feeling of control will be able to indulge themselves in the creation of formidable systems for monitoring operations at the minutest and most intrusive levels of detail.

Imagine that you work for a company called Happy Talk, Inc. Happy Talk runs call centers that do help desk support and telemarketing for their customers. You have been with the company for two years now, and you have been promoted to supervisor. As you walk through the front door the radio frequency identification (RFID) tag in your ID badge registers the exact moment you arrived at work. "Fair's fair," says Neil Heavyhand, the company's president. "Why should I pay for your time if you are not at the office." Every month you get an e-mail showing the cumulative late time you have incurred. When it reaches eight hours, the company deducts a day from your available vacation time.

As you sit down, you open up six small windows across the bottom of your PC screen. These small windows show you a live video feed of the six Happy Talk associates on the team that you supervise. These people each have their call lists and it is up to you to see that they maintain the necessary pace of activity. Above each person's image is a continuously updated display showing his or her hourly productivity. Your dashboard doesn't show you anything about what the rest of the company is doing because "it is none of your damn business," as Mr. Heavyhand says. "You need to keep your eyes on our own associates."

Mr. Heavyhand and his three managers run the show. They recently issued orders that everybody needs to work faster. They have dashboards in their offices that show them lots of stuff like how many calls each team has made and how many calls were successful. You don't want one of them to call you into his office when he notices your numbers slipping. You and the other supervisors are taught to be very watchful of your teams and to quickly identify and remove any associate whose productivity starts to slip. This seemed harsh when you were an associate yourself, but now you understand why it is necessary. "Associates just can't be trusted. They'll goof off every chance they get," you say to yourself. And you've also noticed how important it makes you feel to have those six associates under your thumb. Just imagine how important Mr. Heavyhand must feel.

There will be plenty of variations on this kind of hypercontrolling company in the years ahead. It will be a while until the futility of that type of behavior is widely understood. Between now and then, these hypercontrolling companies offer favorable targets for organizations that have learned a more flexible and decentralized approach to business.

Organizations that know how to create a common worldview for their members enable everyone to participate effectively because everyone understands what is going on. Companies that keep people in the dark and let only a few see the big picture rely excessively on the skill and insights of those few. Organizations that define clear goals and objectives and delegate them to individual business units along with the authority to decide and act as needed can respond intelligently and quickly to changing situations. Companies in which a few make decisions for the many act in slow and clumsy ways. And when they do act, there is little enthusiasm and little follow-through. One should be so lucky as to compete against companies like this.

WHERE IS THE PROFIT IN THE REAL-TIME ECONOMY?

We are living in a time when the economies of individual countries and regions are blending together into a global economy. One of the things that we all notice about this process is the relentless pressure it creates on profit margins. During the decades of the 1980s and 1990s, profit margins were steadily squeezed for most companies on most products. That squeeze has continued. Some companies now often do business at gross margins approaching 10% or less. There is no logical end to this margin pressure. It won't stop at 8%, or 6%, or 4%.

As the markets we serve become global and real time, they become more like stock markets. By this I mean that there is more and more efficient "price discovery," to borrow a term from the commodities traders. The price of an item, any item, is starting to be set in real time by companies such as eBay or Wal-Mart. Soon enough everyone will know the market price for any product, from cars to mobile phones to blue jeans. People will know the market price for basic services such as haircuts, accounting, programming, or child care. To the extent that people pay more than these prices for an item or a service, it will be because they are also receiving a customized mix of value-added services that they want and will pay for. It is in this mix of value-added services that most companies will find the profits they need. Profit on basic products or services alone will be almost nothing.

Most customers consider a handful of value factors in addition to price when they make their buying decisions. They need help in areas such as selecting the best products for their situation, training and post-sales support, packaging and labeling requirements, special delivery requirements, and flexible credit or leasing terms. Once a package of customized offerings in these areas is wrapped around any product, that product ceases to be a commodity.[5]

The successful company will be very good at selecting customers whose needs best match its capabilities and strengths. Companies will have to be more and more particular about the kind of customers they sell to if they hope to make a profit.

If a company's strategy is just to compete on price and go after a broad market, then they had better be the dominant market player. They had better have the lowest cost of sales in their industry. The margins resulting from this kind of strategy are so thin that it takes an enormous amount of volume to make any money. Only the dominant players can succeed because they lower their cost of sales by constantly using their purchasing power to drive very hard bargains with their suppliers.

Since there is by definition room for only one, two, or at most three dominant players in any market, most companies will not be able to compete on price alone. They will instead specialize in the needs of particular kinds of customers, and they will continually evolve with these customers as their needs change. This means that companies will continually evolve their IT infrastructure to support the evolution of their business model.

THOUGHTS ON DESIGNING AND DEPLOYING REAL-TIME SYSTEMS

The real-time enterprise lives in an economy that places most of the profit opportunities in value-added services that are combined with commodity products to create unique offerings. All value-added services are information based because a service has value only if it is tailored accurately to the current needs of specific customers. Today's innovative service becomes tomorrow's standard offering, so the organization is always seeking new service offerings and new ways of delivering those offerings.

What used to be a start-and-stop, once-every-three-or-four-year event to roll out new computer systems must now be an ongoing process of building out and enhancing a company's IT infrastructure. Finding the most responsive and cost effective way to do this is the job of the CIO (chief information officer). The real-time world requires companies to be good at the way they design and use new information systems. Companies that are not good at this will fail just as surely as companies that are not good at sales or new product development.

When building new systems, it is best to get off to a rolling start and then just keep rolling. Map out the big picture that shows where the business is currently and the journey it needs to make over the next few years. Catalog existing application systems, how they interact with each other, and the functionality they provide to people who use them. Look for ways to support the business on its journey by creating needed new systems through building on existing applications.

Application systems must be "highly cohesive and loosely coupled." That means systems should be developed that address well-defined and very focused sets of needs. Avoid the temptation to build all inclusive, Swiss Army knife–type systems. Have different systems talk to each other via standard interfaces called application program interfaces (APIs). These APIs can use interfaces such as ASCII flat files, extensible markup language (XML), or Web services. This technique has come to be called service-oriented architecture (SOA). Using this technique, you can develop new systems by combining pieces and functions from existing systems and only write new programs to deliver brand new functionality. Systems built this way pay for themselves very quickly.

Completion of each application system provides a base from which to build the next system but does not lock the company into any rigid or preset sequence of future system development projects. As each system is completed and goes into production, evaluate changes in the business environment. Update system designs as needed, and build the next system according to what is most needed by the company at that time.

For existing application systems that have proven reliable and useful over the years, it is very effective to combine them with business process management (BPM) systems. BPM systems allow for routine transactions to be processed automatically. They trap transactions that are exceptions and focus people's attention on dealing with just those exceptions. This creates a big jump in business productivity very quickly. It also leads to a rise in profitability since it focuses people's time on handling exceptions, and the exceptions are where the best profit margins are.

Advantage goes to those players who learn to use simple technology and simple tactics extremely well. When you use simple tactics, you can actually remember them in the heat of the moment when you need them. And if you use simple systems, then most of the time they will work as expected and you will be successful. After all is said and done, success is mostly a matter of consistent performance, making fewer errors than your competition, and responding appropriately to opportunities as they present themselves.

EXECUTIVE INSIGHT

THE ART OF INNOVATION AND MOTIVATION

Performing artists have always had to cope with the tension between creativity and control. Artists are forced to do more with less since their funds are limited, so they find ways to be extremely productive. A performance date is not a deadline that can be moved. On a certain day at an advertised time, artists have to show up and perform for an audience every bit as fickle and demanding as any group of customers. What can they teach business about innovation, productivity, and getting things done in the real-time world?

Venetia Stifler is an associate professor at Northeastern Illinois University in the Department of Music and The Dance Program. She has a

PhD in choreography and dance direction from the Union Institute. She is also executive director of the Ruth Page Center for the Arts in Chicago. The center trains dancers and performers, provides office and rehearsal space to a select group of dance companies, and operates a 220-seat theater in its building located in a popular downtown neighborhood. Her dance company, Concert Dance, Inc., performs at venues ranging from the Fringe Festival in Edinburgh, Scotland, to the Ravinia Festival, summer home of the Chicago Symphony Orchestra. She is currently preparing for a tour to Moscow.

When asked how she organizes the work to produce a performance, Venetia replied, "I have to know what I'm trying to do, and I have to know what my performance date is. Then I work backwards and create a timeline. I need to ascertain if it is even doable in the time available." A big part of that calculation is based on whether or not she feels that she will have the artists and the qualified technicians she needs to create and stage the performance.

"If I think the right people are available," she said, "I look at my budget and see if the scope of what I'm doing is within my financial capabilities. If I don't have enough money, then I look at either adjusting the scope or waiting until I have more money." If she does decide to proceed, she gets the people together and starts the rehearsal and production process.

"I believe it was Agnes de Mille who said that for every minute of finished material you need six hours in the studio. Some days it takes a lot of time; other days it comes more quickly." Venetia maintains control of the overall creative direction, but she uses a process that relies heavily on the input of the other artists she is working with. "A successful day in the dance studio starts with everybody showing up prepared. The dancers are warmed up and I have some basic images and movement material to bring to them.

"I explain the images and demonstrate the movement. I expect the dancers to enter into a physical dialog with me. They respond to my ideas, and then some of their movement is stuff that I pick out and elaborate on. We are all working on the same vision; we all participate." The work goes on like this for hours. "I always ask the dancers what images or feelings are coming up for them. Something one person does may spark someone else or spark me. When the movement is right, we all know it; we know when we have created art. I'm the one who decides the steps and the form and the structure of the final composition. But the dancers—who are artists in their own right—have helped me to find the final form."

Keeping people motivated is something Venetia is aware of all the time. "People stay motivated if they all think the dance is based on a good idea. The dancers are very skilled in their technique and at the creative process. Somebody has to be in charge and make the final decisions, but somehow the decisions are easy because we all recognize the good stuff. If more than one person has doubts, I always defer to those doubts and take another look at what is going on.

"Not all choreographers work this way," she said. "The other way to work is someone comes in and says, "5, 6, 7, 8 . . . Do the steps exactly as I say. I'm in control and your job is to do and not think." Venetia explained that she used to work that way when she began as a choreographer. Then she admitted, "It's a very lonely process, though, and it's too hard to create when you're lonely. And sometimes you are really wrong too. I found that I got more cooperation and commitment to the whole project when I used a collaborative process."

Deadlines are serious things in the performing world. "Performers know that once a date has been set and tickets are sold, there is no going back. You simply have to be ready when the date comes." Venetia keeps a very tight timeline on her projects. As things happen and activities slip, she adjusts and compensates immediately. Keeping the rehearsal calendar—making sure the right people are in the right place at the right time—is one of the hardest jobs. "Things are always moving so you have to stay on top of it."

Concerning the qualities of a good leader in the performing arts, Venetia has this to say, "You need to have a clear vision of what you want to do and what you think of as excellent. Then you surround yourself with people who are really good at helping you accomplish your vision." She continued by saying, "Make sure people know what you expect of them. Give them the tools and support they need, and as the project progresses, keep asking if the work is going in the right direction, if it is helping us to do what we want to do and say what we want to say."

In looking at her career, Venetia observes how she has evolved as a leader. "I used to think I had to be responsible for every little thing. Now I realize that creating a performance is an act of trust. You have to trust the people you are working with and let them all add their parts. If you can't trust the people you're working with, then don't work with them.

"When the performance date arrives and the work goes on stage, that's the most important time and also the time when I'm least in control. That's hard," she said. "There are stories about a famous ballerina who went on to have her own company. Once the performance started, she would stand in the wings and shout corrections to her dancers while they were dancing. I've always thought that that kind of failure to let go just makes things worse. If they don't have it after all the rehearsing, they certainly won't get it by being yelled at.

"Businesspeople who think that artists just play at things completely miss the point. Of course we play, that's where the creativity comes from, but then we pull it all together and present it. We do it with almost no money, we don't miss performance dates, we make no excuses, and we put our reputations on the line with every performance. I wonder how many businesspeople could stand up to that kind of pressure?"

ENDNOTES

1. Thoughts attributed to Dee Hock by Howard Smith and Peter Fingar, *Business Process Management: The Third Wave* (Tampa, FL: Meghan-Kiffer Press, 2003), p. 157.
2. For an interesting discussion of this phenomenon, read Howard Rheingold, *Smart Mobs* (Cambridge MA: Basic Books, 2002).
3. A very thoughtful book that discusses behavior similar to swarming behavior is written by Malcolm Gladwell, *The Tipping Point: How Little Things Can Make a Big Difference* (New York: Little, Brown and Company, 2000).
4. Jack Stack, *The Great Game of Business* (New York: Currency/Doubleday, 1992).
5. Tom Peters, *Thriving on Chaos* (New York: Alfred A. Knopf). Peters presents the idea very clearly in this book in a section titled "The Total Product Concept," p. 92.

CHAPTER 11

How to Tell a Winning Project from a Loser

Companies can outsource a lot of functions, but they cannot outsource the activity of looking out for their own best interests. If they do, they wind up in a very weak position where they "depend on the kindness of strangers . . ."[1] The continuous development of new systems to support the real-time enterprise requires that business executives as well as technical managers and system builders become a lot better at evaluating project activities and the likelihood of success on projects as they move through the define, design, and build (DDB) stages.

Business executives who sponsor system development projects and the system builders who lead these projects need a way to assess the projects as they move through the DDB sequence. Business executives and system builders each have different sets of knowledge, concerns, and responsibilities that are important to them when they view a project. So I provide a different checklist of questions for each. The checklists can be used to assess any information technology (IT) development project, and these assessments will reveal quite clearly whether a project is going well or not.

THREE MAIN AREAS OF CONCERN

Answers to these questions will help people connected with a project to make accurate assessments and take appropriate corrective actions. Regardless of whether you are a business executive or a system builder, there are three main areas of concern that need to be investigated:

1. The goodness of the system design
2. The progress made in building the system
3. The competence and confidence of the people on the project

Goodness of the System Design

Notions that good designs must include state-of-the-art technology or complex processing logic are entirely misplaced. The goodness of a particular system design is measured by the combination of two probabilities. The first is the probability that the system will meet the performance criteria that were specified for it to accomplish its business goal or mission. The second probability is the probability that the system can be successfully built.

The best system designs usually do not use state-of-the-art technology or complex processes. This is because newness and complexity tend to introduce uncertainty, which reduces the probability that the system will perform as expected or that it can be built on time and on budget.

The goodness of a system design can be accurately predicted by the extent to which it respects the seven strategic guidelines for designing systems. The more fully a particular design follows these guidelines, the better that design is. If a design does not follow one of these guidelines—as long as it is not the first guideline—it may still be a good design. If a design disregards two guidelines, then there had better be very clear and convincing reasons for doing so. There must also be well-thought-out preparations to compensate for this. If a design disregards three or more of the guidelines, it will fail. The probability of successfully building a system that violates this many guidelines is about the same as the probability of winning the lottery.

Progress Made in Building the System

For a system development project to be successful, it must move along smartly. The pace of progress must be aggressive or the project will tend to lose its focus and begin to wander aimlessly as the world passes it by. An aggressive pace requires two things: (1) that the six tactical principles of running projects be rigorously applied and (2) that effective time-boxing be used on the project.

Senior executives sponsoring a development project are responsible for seeing to it that a qualified full-time leader (system builder) is put in charge.

It is the responsibility of the system builder to then effectively apply the other five tactical principles. There is no convincing reason that any of these principles should be ignored. If you find that one or more of these principles are not being applied, then you need to do everything in your power to correct this. These principles are mutually reinforcing, so if one of them is not being applied that creates a dynamic that will start to undermine the application of all the others.

The second requirement—that effective time-boxing be used—means that the activities of each project team should be organized to follow a clear define–design–build sequence. The activities in each phase need to be completed within the time boxes and budgets that are appropriate to each phase. This means that the system builder works with the project team leaders to set the time boxes. Then the project teams keep up the pace to meet these deadlines.

Competence and Confidence of People on the Project

People charged with developing new systems must be competent and confident in order to succeed. If they are competent but lack confidence, they will have trouble. If they are not competent but full of confidence, they will have even more trouble. People must both know how to do the job being asked of them, and they must have good leadership.

Two things can measure the presence of these qualities. The first is the degree to which the people working on the project can efficiently use the six core techniques. For the people who lead projects and project teams and for the individuals on the project teams, technique is everything. The system builder and the team leaders need to understand and know when to employ each of the six core techniques. They must be competent in all of the techniques and masters of a few of them. The individuals on the project teams must be competent in or masters of the specific core techniques that they will need for their roles on the team. It is the efficient use of these core techniques that allows project teams to get things done within the aggressive time boxes needed for a successful project.

The second thing is the degree to which the system builder and the team leaders are capable of demonstrating the skills for designing systems and leading projects. Those skills are somewhat subjective but not entirely. After a period of watching someone in action, most observers can make a fairly accurate assessment of the degree to which that person possesses the design and leadership skills (even if the observers do not themselves have those skills). When the project leaders and team leaders have these skills, good system designs will emerge, effective leadership will happen, and there will be a visible air of confidence among the people on the project.

CHECKLIST FOR THE BUSINESS EXECUTIVE

Goodness of System Design

Ask yourself and the system builder in charge of the project the following questions. It is best, if you can, to ask these questions in the first two to six weeks (the define phase) of the project.

What is the business goal or mission of the project?   In two sentences or less, state the action the company is going to take and state the desired result of that action.

The *goal* is the target, the destination the project is supposed to reach. If you do not know where you are going, then you will never get there. If you cannot clearly and simply state the goal that the system is supposed to accomplish, then neither you nor anyone else really knows what the system is supposed to do. Figure this out or stop the project. For further explanation see

- Chapter 8: "Applied Strategy and Tactics" and "The Define–Design–Build Process"
- Chapter 9: "Define—The Framework for Action" and "Defining the Project Goal"

What are the performance criteria that the system is supposed to meet?   State what requirements the system will meet in four areas:

1. Business operations
2. Customer expectations
3. Financial performance
4. Company learning and improvement

These performance measures are the specific measures that will determine whether the system is a success or not. Make sure that you know what they are and that the people designing and building the system know what they are. Otherwise, you will get a system that does not do what you want. For further explanation see

- Chapter 9: "Defining the Project Goal" and "Creating the Strategy"
- Chapter 10: "The Great Game of Business" and "Harnessing the Self-Adjusting Feedback Loop"

As an experienced businessperson, do you believe that a system that meets the preceding performance requirements will in fact accomplish the business goal that you are striving for?   If you have a feeling that some important performance requirements have been left out, then add them in before the project gets any farther along, but make sure that you do not add requirements that are not strictly necessary to accomplish the business goal. When the performance requirements become too broad, this will result in increased system complexity and lower the chances that the system can be successfully built. For further explanation see

- Chapter 2: "General Systems Theory" and "Six Sigma"
- Chapter 3: "Complex Adaptive Systems" and "System Dynamics"
- Chapter 9: "The Conceptual System Design" and "The Decision to Proceed or Not Proceed"

What are the existing computer systems in your company (that work well enough) that are being leveraged in the design for the new computer system?   The new system should leverage the strengths of systems and procedures that already exist in your company. That way the new system can focus on delivering new capabilities instead of just replacing something that already exists that works well enough. If you decide to replace everything and build from a clean slate, you had better be prepared for the considerable extra time and expense involved and be sure that it is worth it. For further explanation see

- Chapter 6: "Toward a New IT Strategy" and "IT Infrastructure for the Agile Real-Time Organization"
- Chapter 8: "Strategic Guidelines for Designing Systems"

How does the overall design for the new system break down into a set of self-contained subsystems that can each operate on their own and provide value?   Large computer systems that cost a lot of money are really made up of a bunch of smaller systems that all combine to create the large system. Your company should be able to build each subsystem independently of the others. That way if one subsystem runs into problems, work on the others can still proceed. As subsystems are completed they need to be put into production as soon as possible and begin paying back the company for the expense of building them. If all subsystems must be complete before any subsystem can be put to use, then that is a very risky all-or-nothing system design. Change it. For further explanation see

- Chapter 6: "Quickly Build Systems That Are Good, Not Perfect"
- Chapter 9: "Define Project Objectives"
- Chapter 10: "Thoughts on Designing and Deploying Real-Time Systems"

How accurate is the cost-benefit analysis for the new system? Have the business benefits been overstated? Would the project still be worth doing if the business benefits were only half of those predicted? Cost-benefit calculations usually understate costs and overstate benefits. You are the one best able to judge the validity of the benefits—do you believe they are accurate? The bigger and riskier the system development project, the larger the benefits must be to justify the risk and expense. Do not spend more on a system than it is worth. For further explanation see

- Chapter 8: "The Define–Design–Build Process" and "Benefits of the Define–Design–Build Process"
- Chapter 9: "Create Initial Plan and Budget"

Who is the senior technical person in charge of the project—the system builder? How has this person demonstrated that his or her system design and project leadership skills are appropriate to the demands of the project?   If you do not have a qualified system builder in charge of the project, it will fail from lack of direction—management by committee will not work. If this person does not have the necessary design and leadership skills, he or she is not qualified and must be replaced no matter what other skills he or she may possess. For further explanation see

- Chapter 4: "What is Leadership?"
- Chapter 7: "The System Builder," "Designing Systems," and "Leading Projects"

Ask the system builder to explain to you which of the strategic guidelines for designing systems have been followed and which have not. For those that have not been followed, why not? If all seven of the strategic guidelines are followed, the design of the system you are developing is very good. It is acceptable if one of the guidelines is not followed—any one except the first one. If two of the guidelines are not followed, there had better be VERY good reasons, and extra precautions need to be taken to compensate for the increased risk. What are these precautions? If more than two of the guidelines are not followed, then the design is fatally flawed—the system cannot be built on time or on budget if it can even be built at all. For further explanation see

- Chapter 8: "Strategic Guidelines for Designing Systems"
- Chapter 9: "Apply the Seven Strategic Guidelines" and "Executive Insight: Two Wins, a Lose, and a Draw"

Progress Made Developing the System

Ask these questions once the conceptual system design and initial budget have been agreed upon—the end of the define phase. Ask yourself, the system builder, and the people on the project team the following questions as the project moves through the design and build phases.

Is there a project plan and budget in place? Do people pay attention to the project plan? Is there a project office group that provides people with regular and accurate updates to the plan and the budget? Multimillion-dollar system development projects involve a lot of people and stretch across some period of time. The project plan is the central co-ordinating instrument that tells everybody at any given time exactly what they are supposed to be doing. If the plan is not kept current, the people on the project have no way to effectively coordinate their work with each other. The system builder will lose track of the details. Delays, cost overruns, and confusion will result. People will lose control of the project budget—they will not know how much has been spent to date or how much more is required to finish. When this happens, the project goes into a death spiral. For further explanation see

- Chapter 9: "Creation of the Detailed Plan and Budget," "The Project Office," and "Executive Insight: Two Wins, a Lose, and a Draw"

Are the teams working on each subsystem organizing their work into a clearly defined design phase and a build phase? Are these phases getting done within the appropriate time boxes and budgets? Or do time boxes keep expanding and budgets keep growing? The project team working on each subsystem should spend one to three months and no more to create a detailed design and system prototype (design phase). The detailed design should then be turned into a working system within two to six months (build phase). If things take longer than this, that means the project is moving too slowly and it will lose momentum and drift. It is the system builder's responsibility to keep things organized and moving—make sure this person is in place and is capable. For further explanation see

- Chapter 5: "The Agile Real-Time Corporation"
- Chapter 8: "The Define-Design-Build Process," "Benefits of the Define-Design-Build Process," and "Managing the Encounter With Complexity"
- Chapter 9: "The Role of the System Builder," "Lead by Staying Involved," and "Executive Insight: Two Wins, a Lose, and a Draw"

Ask the system builder to explain to you how the six tactical principles for running projects are being applied to the running of this project. Do you believe the answers you hear? Can the system builder explain this clearly using plain language or does he or she resort to the use of "tech talk" and jargon? A qualified person can give you straight answers. The system builder is in effect your general contractor who is running the job. This person can make or break the project—get a new one if you need to. For further explanation see

- Chapter 8: "Tactical Principles for Running Projects" and "Executive Insight: Using Information Technology to Grow the Business"

Spot-check the project plan and budget from time to time. Have the system builder review the current, updated project plan with you and explain the situation on the project as of that week. Have the system builder show you the money spent to date on each subsystem and the estimate for remaining time and budget to complete each subsystem. Do you believe the answers you hear? Can the system builder explain the situation clearly without tech talk or jargon? How does the most recent estimate of time and budget compare to the original estimate for time and budget? Is it still worth the cost to complete the project? For further explanation see

- Chapter 9: "The Decision to Proceed or Not Proceed," "The Project Office," and "Figure 9.5: Build Phase"

Competence and Confidence of People on the Project

Ask the following questions of yourself, the system builder, and the people on the project teams.

Ask each of the project teams to make a presentation to you at the end of their design phase, where they show you the design specifications they have created. Ask them to walk you through the process flow diagrams and the logical data model for the subsystem they are responsible for. Ask them to show you the user interface, the technical architecture diagrams, and the system prototype. Can they tell you how this system will deliver the business benefits that are listed in the cost-benefit analysis? Do the design specifications make any sense? Do the people on the team know what they are talking about? For further explanation see

- Chapter 7:"The Core Techniques"
- Chapter 9: "The Decision to Proceed or Not Proceed" and "Design Phase Deliverables"

Are the project team members as confident in the success of the project as the project team leaders? Are the team leaders as confident as the system builder? If people feel they have the right skills and believe they have a good system design to work from, they will be confident in their ability to build the system. There is a problem somewhere if people at every level of the project do not share and reflect this confidence. If people are trying to transfer onto the project, that indicates people have confidence it will succeed. If people are transferring off the project or leaving the company, that indicates people have no confidence and expect it to fail. For further explanation see

- Chapter 4: "Change Creates Fear—Why Companies Fail"
- Chapter 9: "Creation of the Detailed Project Plan and Budget" and "The Decision to Proceed or Not Proceed"

Checklist for the System Builder

Goodness of System Design

If you are the system builder leading the project or you are one of the project team leaders first ask yourself all of the system design questions listed previously. The senior business executive sponsoring the project will ask you these questions. Make sure you can give clear and accurate answers to each of these questions. Then ask yourself the following additional questions.

How exactly does each feature of the new system support the improvements in the business process flows that are needed to deliver the benefits that will pay for the system?   Each feature of the system you are designing or building should directly contribute to delivering the business benefits that justify building the system. Remove all system features that do not directly contribute to delivering the desired business benefits. For further explanation see

- Chapter 6: "Using Technology to Support the Real-Time Enterprise," "Act: Improve Existing Procedures or Create New Procedures," and "Quickly Build Systems That Are Good, Not Perfect"
- Chapter 7: "What Organizations Need From Information Technology" and "Designing Systems"
- Chapter 10: "Thoughts on Designing and Deploying Real-Time Systems"

What kind of feedback do you get from the businesspeople who have seen the user interface? Do they like it? Can you imagine yourself using and liking the system you are developing?   If you included people who will use the system in the process of creating the user interface they will like what has been designed. If you found the simple, underlying patterns in the workflows that the system will support, then the user interface should closely fit those patterns and be pretty easy for people to learn and to use. The better the user interface design, the easier it will be for people to learn and use the system. For further explanation see

- Chapter 6: "Orient: Turning Data into Information"
- Chapter 7: "Designing Systems"

Have you have found an elegantly simple combination of technology and business process to get the job done?   You know you have found elegant simplicity when you find a small set of technology and procedures that can be combined in different ways to build all the subsystems called for in the overall system design. If you are using different technology to build each subsystem, you have not yet found the elegantly simple combination you need. The encounter with complexity is the central challenge of the system building profession. Simpler designs get built. Complex designs become shipwrecks on the uncharted reefs of their own complexity. For further explanation see

- Chapter 5: "The Agile Real-Time Corporation"
- Chapter 6: "Toward a New IT Strategy" and "IT Infrastructure for the Agile Real-Time Organization"
- Chapter 9: "The Role of the System Builder"

What are the test results you get from benchmarking the prototype you built of the proposed technical architecture? Why do you believe that the hardware and software specified in the system technical design will perform as desired and carry the load that the system will need to handle?   Do not accept the benchmark test results provided by hardware and software vendors as it is not clear whether those results were obtained under conditions that are relevant to your situation. Set up an adequate test environment and see for yourself how the technology works. Do not be afraid to change technology components if they are unable to perform as advertised. You are responsible for selecting the right technology—use only the technology you are confident in. For further explanation see

- Chapter 7: "The Core Techniques"
- Chapter 9: "Design—Workflow and System Design" and "The Design Process"

Progress Made Developing the System

First, ask yourself the progress questions listed previously that the senior executives will ask you. Make sure you can answer clearly and accurately. Then ask these additional questions.

Are you tracking the project at the task level of detail? Are your tasks all defined as taking one week or less to finish? *Project tasks are simply either started, not started, or complete.* If you are using the "percentage complete" method of tracking progress on multiweek project tasks you are living in a fool's paradise. All large tasks will be reported as the expected percentage complete until the last week, when they will suddenly be found to need a whole lot more time to finish. This will make you will look very clumsy as you miss deadlines and stagger from one unexpected problem to the next. For further explanation see

- Chapter 3: "System Dynamics"
- Chapter 8: "Tactical Principles for Running Projects" and "Managing the Encounter with Complexity"
- Chapter 9: "The System Blueprints"

How soon are you able to see emerging problems that can cause deadlines to be missed or cost overruns to occur? How effectively are you able to take corrective actions to keep the project on time and on budget? If you are tracking the project at the task level of detail and if the project office staff is doing its job you will have updated plans and budgets every week. The more accurate your plans and budgets are, the sooner you can see problems arising. The sooner you see problems coming, the more time you have to do something about it. When problems do arise, you can respond with some combination of spending more time, spending more money, or cutting the scope of the subsystem that has run into trouble. For further explanation see

- Chapter 7: "Leading Projects"
- Chapter 9: "The Project Office" and "Lead by Staying Involved"

Are there regular weekly meetings in which the system builder and the team leaders meet in person to review project plans and budgets and discuss problems and responses? In order to maintain the aggressive pace of work called for by a successful project, it is very important to have regular weekly meetings with the people who lead the project teams. These meetings can be productive only if project plans and budgets are updated before each meeting. Problem resolution will be effective if people focus on current issues and avoid discussing personalities and bemoaning past decisions. For further explanation see

- Chapter 9: "The Project Office" and "Lead by Staying Involved"

Are you delivering subsystems or system components that can be put to use by the company every 30 to 90 days? What are the people who started using these subsystems saying about them? How do they improve the workflow process? You need to create momentum and positive expectations on the project. One of the best ways to do this is to make sure that you deliver something of value as soon and as often as you can. As the company puts these deliverables to use, you will get valuable feedback and you will also be seen as someone who is helping the company succeed, not just spending its money. For further explanation see

- Chapter 8: "Tactical Principles for Running Projects," "Managing the Encounter with Complexity," and "Executive Insight: Using Information Technology to Grow the Business"
- Chapter 10: "Thoughts on Designing and Deploying Real-Time Systems"

Competence and Confidence of People on the Project

If you are the system builder, ask these questions of yourself, the team leaders, and the people on the project teams.

Do you feel competent in the use of the core techniques? Can you review and critique the design specification documents produced by these techniques: process flow diagrams, data models, system architecture schematics, and object models? Can you discuss specific details in the design specifications with the project team members who did the work to create them? The core techniques are the knowledge base for the profession of systems building. These techniques continue to evolve so stay current with them. You will need to know how and when to use these techniques to get things done quickly and efficiently. These techniques are powerful weapons for confronting complexity, for breaking it into smaller pieces, and then resolving each piece (divide and conquer). For further explanation see

- Chapter 7: "The Core Techniques"
- Chapter 9: "The Role of the System Builder," "The System Blueprints," and "System Test and Rollout"

Are the team leaders hands-on people who lead their teams by example? Do they assign to themselves some of the hardest work that their team has to do because they are the most qualified to do it?   Leaders say, "Do as I do" and "Follow me." Administrators or managers say, "Do as I say" and "I'm right behind you." Leaders do development work and managers do operations work—do not confuse the two and the kind of work that they do. If managers are asked to do development work, it will not get done quickly if it gets done at all. For further explanation see

- Chapter 4: "What Is Leadership?"
- Chapter 8: "Tactical Principles for Running Projects"

Are there people on the project teams who know both the business operations being supported and the technology being used? Do these people know how to use the core techniques that are relevant to the job that they must do for the success of the project?   Make sure that each project team is composed of people who are knowledgeable and competent in both the business operations and in the use of the technology chosen to support those operations. Make sure that these people are each trained in the use of the core techniques they need. This is the only way that they will be able to do consistently competent (and sometimes brilliant) work within the time boxes allocated to each activity. For further explanation see

- Chapter 7: "Designing Systems" and "The Core Techniques"
- Chapter 9: "Design—Workflow and System Design," "The Role of the System Builder," and "The Design Process"

What is the level of morale and optimism of the people on the project?   Do people want to transfer onto the project or are people finding ways to leave the project? People want to be part of success and they distance themselves from failure. They may know something about

the project that you do not—pay attention to this. For further explanation see

- Chapter 7: "Leading Projects"
- Chapter 10: "The Art of Innovation and Motivation"

EXECUTIVE INSIGHT

THE CHIEF INFORMATION OFFICER AS SUCCESSFUL BUSINESS EXECUTIVE

Sheleen Quish is vice president and chief information officer (CIO) at U.S.
Can Corporation. U.S. Can is an $800 million company that operates
plants in North America and Europe. It manufactures containers such as
aerosol spray cans, paint and general use cans, custom and specialty
cans, and plastic containers for the consumer packaged-goods industry.

"People are tired of having the CIO talk as if they are a prima donna,"
said Sheleen. "Y2K was our swan song. We made a big deal out of it
and then nothing happened. Whether we admit it or not, our credibility
was severely damaged. A lot of executives now think information technology is pretty easy and that it doesn't deserve a 'C-Level' position."
Just knowing about technology in and of itself is no longer a sufficient
reason to be part of senior management, she said. She believes the
role of the CIO is changing and a new set of skills is needed as the person in this role must become a senior businessperson instead of a senior technologist.

The CIO is often a person who is in an awkward position. This is because the IT profession has made a series of mistakes over the last
decade or so. "CIOs are often not effective communicators. They tend
to be very modest and they aren't good at promoting themselves. When
things go wrong, they don't get out in front of the situation," Sheleen
explained. "When I see things not going well, I'm out in front right
away. I take responsibility first and then I issue alerts. I let people know
what's going on. I want to be the one who controls the story. And when
things go well, I'm there too.

"Also, we haven't done a good job of nurturing the next generation.
We haven't given technical people a good 360-degree view of business. Some days I don't even know if there is a next generation of
people who aspire to be CIOs." There is a real lack of understanding

about business practices on the part of technical people. In addition, there is a lot of misinformation and simplistic notions on the part of business people about what technology can do. "For instance, the notion that you are going to run your whole company on a collection of packaged software applications like ERP or CRM is pretty naive.

"One of the things IT people do that hurts us in the executive ranks is all the talking and thinking about IT governance. Because we IT people have made such a big deal about it we have isolated and separated ourselves from other executives. CFOs [chief financial officers] and COOs [chief operating officers] don't do this—asking other executives to validate their projects. CIOs have executive steering committees that get to chew over every IT project. We are the only department in the company that has to endure that kind of review. Why don't the business leaders have to justify what they want to do that happen to require IT support as opposed to us justifying the IT projects as a stand-alone effort?"

Sheleen observed that there is another way for CIOs to do their job. "I have a whole other model in mind. It is me as a businessperson managing costs and delivering resources that the business needs. CIOs run their own business like the COO does. Give me a budget and I'll invest it wisely to support various areas of the company. I'll market my services to the business and be judged on my deliverables. You have to come up with an offering so good that other executives will come to you to get it."

To illustrate this point, she described what she did as CIO at a previous organization and what she is doing in her present company. "When I was CIO at BlueCross BlueShield of Kentucky I created an electronic claim submission and electronic payment offering and then sold this to hospitals and doctors' offices. We became a profit center. We sold them hardware, licenses for our proprietary software solution, training, and support. We showed people how to manage their cash flow and at the same time reduced our parent company's costs and motivated the right behavior from the providers. It was a win–win. Here at U.S. Can I envision the development of an offering to help our customers solve their supply chain visibility needs. We can deliver the information they need at the right time and in the right format to enable them to make better decisions. This will provide us both with a collaboration vehicle that streamlines communication, reduces the time and effort to enter orders, and allows for the maximum flexibility."

The CIO needs to be someone who can get things done and deliver systems solutions. Sheleen feels that effectively overseeing the design and build of systems is a core skill of the CIO. "The business problem needs to be well defined in business terms. The value add that a business savvy CIO brings is the ability to step back in an objective role and facilitate the definition of alternatives and drive toward a winning solution. You need to know what is going to change from a process and technology perspective by tackling a project. You need to know the outcome that is desired and how it will be measured. Then you sit down with programmers and business analysts who know your existing systems and you tell them what the business needs."

"You ask them to come up with some approaches to meet those needs. They will come up with different ideas and when they can work through the issues and come to agreement on a solution then you know that they get it. When people know what needs to be done, the actual coding is not that hard." Sheleen believes that "the good business analyst is the future of the IT function. The business analyst is the person who can match technology with business needs. Good analysts are the communicators and facilitators who help a project team to work through the issues and come to agreements."

I asked her what thoughts she has about career management that she would offer to other CIOs or to people who want to become CIOs. "When I have gotten into trouble it was not due to any particular project as it was just not being part of the executive team. That is the most career-limiting factor going. You need to consciously size up an organization and see if and how you fit in. Respect other people's expertise—the world doesn't revolve around IT. Recognize that the company's problems are your problems and that you are responsible for solving them by working with other executives."

Here is a self-test Sheleen recommends that CIO's take to evaluate their value within their company. It is a good tool to figure out how much longer you can be successful in your current role. Prerequisite: Be completely honest with yourself and don't assume anything.

1. What specific business problems have you helped find solutions for in the last two years? List them in business terms, and recap the solution and the total cost. Identify what changed: people, process, technology. Identify measurable actual results versus expected results. Was the project done on time and within budget? Did the business organization recognize the value of the final solution? Did anyone celebrate the success?

2. If you asked the process owners in these functional areas to answer the same questions how close would their answers be to your answers?

3. If a relationship counselor sat you and one of your business colleagues down and talked to you about how you live and work together, would you be in a compatible, open relationship, a challenged relationship, or a dysfunctional relationship? Can this relationship be saved; are both parties willing to work on making it better?

Endnote

1. These are the famous words spoken by the vulnerable character Blanche DuBois in the play by Tennessee Williams, *A Streetcar Named Desire* (New York: Viking Penguin, 1947).

Index